Foreword

"...James Bourne's English language translation of Maurice Magre's lost masterpiece is a literary event of the first degree. This epic gothic fantasy, reminiscent of the very best of Tolkien, Mervyn Peake or Robert E. Howard, is all the more powerful for its basis in meticulously researched historical fact and Magre's intimate knowledge of the landscape and culture his words so richly evoke. His first person account of the last stand of the Cathars is vast, vivid and noble, his incantatory prose poetic and savage by turns, his vision and message uncompromising in its purity. 'The Blood of Toulouse' opens a window into a dark, medieval world lit by the holy hellfire of the Inquisition and illuminated by timeless dreams and desires making it essential reading for aficionados of the fantastic as well as all those who would seek to understand this little known but pivotal turning point in European history, the apocalyptic chain of events that lead to the death of the age of chivalry..." Richard Stanley

I'd like to thank Martin Lowe, John Redhead, Melissa Baird and Joanna Bourne for proofreading and great support.
I'd like to thank Richard Stanley for giving me 'Le Sang de Toulouse', for inspiring me to translate it, and along with Miss Scarlet for helping me with all manner of post translation pep ups.

Much of my time translating this wonderful epic was spent at my desk in the Pyrenees with my baby girl wrapped in a blanket on my knee. She listened as I read it over in French then in English, watched as my fingers tapped on the keys and is now testimony that this project has taken a very long time to complete. On this note I thank Mette for her love, patience and understanding.

A very special thanks to Joanna Bourne who created the wonderful woodcuts that embellish the pages of this book and lastly to Ian Chapman for the fabulous front cover.

0

Preface

Glory to the sun-blessed earth, stretching from the sea where the Moorish galleys' sail, to the lands of pines and on, till the endless ocean!

Glory to the Garonne, emerging from Pyrenean springs and holding specters of Aran's light in their bewitched waters, giving the vines their drunken dwarf appearance and the poplar its powers of meditation!

Glory to the men of Oc who knew the truth about God's three divine principles thirteen hundred years after Jesus was born. They knew how the soul passed through the doors of successive deaths and died for having known it.

Glory to Toulouse, the city with its twenty-nine gates, which Tolus, Japhets grandson, founded. The city built in red stone, unconquerable, like the hearts of the heretics.

I want to tell you of the unbelievable scenes* that I witnessed. The joyful and criminal acts I accomplished. The worthy prowess that is my glory and the desolation and beauty I contemplated without dying.

In those times women were more beautiful than nowadays. They had a spring in their steps and the joy of freedom. The Garonne flowed wider on its bed of sand and pink stones and the sun cut a finer silhouette on the heights of the ochre Saracen towers.

Toulouse was full of poets and men of letters. There was a Jewish school of medicine and a college of Arabic philosophy.
The Grande route du Midi via Saint-Gilles and Frejus was a pathway to the Orient.

1

Caravans brought perfumes and spices from Damas, carpets from Samarkand and musical instruments that no one could play, from mysterious China.

Now there are no more marvelous silks. There are no more Occitan singers. No more Arabic philosophers! By as a direct consequence, nature becomes less magnificent in its profusion of trees and in the colors of its sun, as man becomes more evil.

The things I am going to say will make you cry, for nothing brings tears like beauty that is forever lost, like intelligence, which is extinguished. Tears however, are more useful to man than joy and the salt that they possess is an element of virility.

If you are astounded that I have been able to bear such calamities and survive, know that I was chosen to tell this tale. My mission is to recognize in the brightness of their eyes, those who need to hear me, those who will keep the memory and will in turn, tell the tale.

Stories written on parchments are destroyed by those who wish to maintain ignorance, but the word falls on souls, just like the doves that come from afar and land, only to leave again. This is a form of justice. Evil and hatred cannot stand face to face as the spoken word dissolves them by the light it emanates, just like a necromancer's pointed blade annihilates the cloud of evil spirits.

I will also call up the dead. They don't sleep in peace, as the Church's prayers would have us believe. There are no psalms sung and there are no ceremonies that stop the dead creatures from haunting the places where they caused pain.

De Montfort is there, the evil one, more hermetically sealed in his hatred than in his coffin. Foulque is there, the hypocrite, eternally holding his pepper-laced fingernails to his eyes, in order to cry false tears. Raymond* is there, the indecisive, tossing coins to end his indecision.

Here is the vile Tancrède with his donkey ears and owl eyes, who had a taste for causing suffering and bragged about inventing an instrument of torture. Here is Dominique, the bald one, and Innocent with his peacock feathered tiara.

I show the faces that were hidden under hoods and the leprosy that bursts behind the velvet doublet. The majorities amongst the strong ones of yesteryear are only quivering shadows and gather round gently when I make a sign.

There are also the uncountable victims, those that suffered patiently, those that became yellow with rage and those that fought for their rights. My memories call to them with the sword of their wars, the sex of their desires and the book of their dead belief. If there are some Parfaits who liberated themselves through pardon and who escaped the terrestrial cycle, may they give my thoughts consideration, strength to my voice and breath to my chest, so that, through the magical mold of syllables, I may pour the gold of truth.

�֎

* At the beginning of the XIII century, the south of France was ravaged by a crusade that Pope Innocent III preached against the Albigensian heretics, the goal was to dispossess Raymond VI, count of Toulouse.

* The Count of Toulouse was the most powerful Lord in Christianity after the Saint-Gilles of France and his estates prospered with exceptional freedoms and great civilization.

The Blood of Toulouse

Part One

I

Resounding bells form the origins of my life. I woke one night longing to hear that sound of resonating bronze. In those days, my blood pumped through my veins with such vigor that I could achieve any zealous ambition I set myself. I looked at the cross-shaped opening, chiseled out of the wall of my monastic cell. There was only darkness outside and I could barely distinguish the outline of the Sedours Mountain. The waters of the Ariège softly lapped on the abbey stones. I opened the door that led to the cloisters and listened. The monastery was silent. A line of pillars stretched out before me, like the regularity of a nocturnal obsession. I took two or three steps and started to laugh raucously, without reason, my soul bursting with effervescent joy.

I had made no plans. I could easily have found some lay clothing and a bag of provisions, if I had the faintest idea what I was about to do. I've always thought that the soul meditates whilst sleeping and takes irrevocable decisions to which the awakened person is bound to obey. I felt so weightless I began to run.

Above the cloister's porch, a lit window stared out into the darkness like a red eye.

It was the guest of honor's room, a room full of frescoes, where the papal envoy Pierre de Castelnau* was resting after his arrival in the monastery that evening.

He was already awake, although I suspected that he had not yet been to sleep. I wondered if insomnia was part of the turpitude reserved for those tormented by remorse. Was my innocent soul's sleep like a clear sky at night? I remembered the anxiety that I had felt under the limpid gaze of de Castelnau's waxy face as he turned towards me; this memory and the contempt of his greasy diplomacy suddenly overtook me and doubled my resolve. With my left hand I grabbed the tail of my robe so that I might cross the cloister quicker and reach the tower that held the bell with its all-mighty sound.

It was nearly a year since I had become a novice in this abbey, founded by a saint called Martial. It lies near the little town of Mercus, on the banks of the Ariège. In vain, my father, the famous Rochemaure, had begged me not to put on that sombre monk's habit that, according to him, I should throw on the compost as quickly as possible.

He had always shown a deep intuition when speaking of my character and future, often punctuating his speech with a gesture he had gleaned from his work in cathedral constructions. He looked as if he was drawing a steeple cleaving the sky.

"You will never do anything sensible," he said. He would hit his forehead making it understood that my intelligence lacked equilibrium. "One must build one's soul like one builds a cathedral. The steeple can only be high if the foundations are buried like roots in the earth."

He had wanted me to start an apprenticeship at the brotherhood where he was the master. Unfortunately the ecclesiastical fraternities had just received an order from the count of Toulouse stopping laymen from building. So he had sent me to learn fencing with a Florentine master who taught outdoors, in the Place des Carmes. I had an aptitude for swordsmanship and rapidly excelled at it. It didn't last though. I became friends with Samuel Manassès, the doctors' son and he introduced me to poetry and Greek philosophy. I soon perfected Greek and learned Arabic so that I could read Plato.

For the only texts by the great sage that one could find in Toulouse were Arabic translations, brought from Seville by Jewish men of letters.

It was then that I met the monk Petrus. He lived as a beggar and he lived well. It was thanks to his ability to insult people so pleasantly that he was rewarded with a meal, or money. At the crossroads he preached against the wealth of the bishops and the debauchery of the lords. I liked him at first for his leanness, for obesity in a man has always inspired my disgust.

We chatted under the flowering pergolas that used stand beside the tour du Bazacle. Like all too many beautiful and agreeable things, they were obliterated in the wars. I was easily the most eloquent of my peers due to that admirable gift of speech that I had received in abundance. My aptitude in discourse was such that at the age of seven I harangued the boys at the corner of the rue du Taur and the place Saint-Sernin. During our discussions I could see surprise in Petrus' eyes, a lightning bolt of admiration that he disguised as stuttering or ignorance. I thought I was easily winning the metaphysical discussions we had every evening. Not so. It was he who triumphed. This is what he did.

He thought that by clever manipulation of prayer one could communicate directly with Jesus Christ. One needed patience and method and if you had both you could communicate with him on a daily basis. Petrus himself, despite his humility, lived under his surveillance. Several times, when he was out drinking in bawdy taverns a stooped and bearded peasant of simple attire came to sit opposite him and gently removed the glass from his hand.

"Who is this strange peasant?" He had asked his companions.

They had simply laughed for they saw no one. Petrus knew, with certainty in his heart that Jesus in person had appeared to him. Nevertheless he continued drinking, perhaps a little less, for he reasoned that only excess is reprehensible.

6

He promised me that if I prayed with the necessary fervor, I too would be in direct communication with Jesus. I was naive enough to ask how long it would take.

"About a month," he said before adding, "on the condition that you stop your insane discourses!" These words were pronounced with the pious aim of tempering my arrogance, for envy was unknown to him.

In Toulouse much was spoken about Martial, and the vow of silence he took and kept for five years. I set out immediately towards his abbey, where I knew that St Benoit's rules were applied with vigor.

This rule demands that the candidate's vocation is tested upon arrival. The door has to shut three times, with a day's interval in between each time. I stayed three days under the July sun, which was stronger than usual, and under the clear nights it became maliciously cold when the mountains began cutting themselves out of the azure.

I did not complain as I had hope in my heart. However I thought I had noticed a mocking irony in the porter's expression and I was resolute in coaxing him out to teach him a lesson with my stick. Even so, on the fourth morning, both panels of the door opened with solemnity and it was the Prior who, as befits his stature, came to greet me. I forgot the porter's cajoling and fell to my knees. However, it was not the revered Martial' sandal that I kissed in the dust. He had died a while ago and I hadn't heard about it. Instead, I found myself in front of a fat northern abbot sent by the head-abbey who spoke to me in that hard and distasteful dialect that is spoken in Paris.

Sympathy and antipathy circulate around people in waves almost visible to the naked eye. Behind the abbot's smile I noticed a mocking contempt when I told him modestly that I was from Toulouse. When I added, lowering my eyes, that I was the son of Rochemaure, famous master of the brotherhood of cathedral builders, he pretended not to know the name.

7

He raised his limp hands, unctuous to the touch, in a gesture of false kindness.

I protected myself by retreating into silence as if surrounded by an imaginary wall. It became known that I didn't say anything because I had nothing to say. All the most degrading and menial tasks were given to me. I didn't complain about emptying the slops, feeding the pigs in their yard, or standing guard in the fields to fight off the bands of marauders. I suffered from not finding the silence that favors the divine presence. In amongst the chattering and quibbling monks, I was transported into a world of speech without beauty. The abbot was au-fait with all the jurisdictions of the land and buried himself in law. Instead of prayers, the novices learned by heart the Justinian laws, and then recited them to a plaintiff rhythm. We copied onto parchments the common laws and precedents of all countries. We discussed the decrees of parliament, the regal ordinances, and the judgments of the consular tribunals. I took refuge in my inner monastery with its thousand cloisters and the thousand sanctuaries of my soul and waited for Petrus' promised apparition. Instead, the peasants I saw were vulgar mountain folk, who came to sell their fruit and vegetables, and their form, devoid of any transparency, was made of the thickest matter.

I suffered most however from the pitiful smile I saw on the abbots' mouth when he looked at me. One becomes stupid amongst those who consider you so; in the same way that one grows amongst those who believe you are capable of growth.

This masquerade lasted until the night of the bell. That evening, amidst great pomp and ceremony Pierre de Castelnau arrived. He came from Toulouse where he had repressed the heresy and on route to Foix decided he wanted to catch up with his friend, the abbot of Mercus. I had heard such terrible things said about the repression that I didn't want to believe them. From the time I knew him to be in the abbey I felt a strange apprehension. I had been sent to the stables to take care of the escort's horses, and as I crossed the cloisters to go to the dining hall, the abbot and his friend suddenly confronted me.

In spite of his mediocre stature, he was rather imposing. He was adorned by a crimson Dalmatia on a red silken robe, a belt encrusted with rubies and his gloves and shoes were the color of fire. From the top of a large triangular hat, a hood fell to his shoulders, whose purple hue accentuated the mattness of his waxen face and adamantine, yet, lifeless blue eyes.

Was this a foreboding of things to come? My heart began thumping in my chest. Pierre de Castelnau had stopped and I saw him examine me with infinite curiosity. His gaze fell on my hands and arms, filthy up to the elbows, from the manure I had just been turning. He asked me in that squawking northern drawl. I didn't understand him. The tone indicated that he was saying any old thing, devoid of importance, merely in an attempt to present goodwill in spite of his malice.

Neither of us knew that in that solemn second the first link in an unparalleled chain of horror was forged. Between the papal envoy in his red dress and this miserable monks' servant, an occult bond was established that could only be broken by death. From this link an inconceivable drama would spring, causing the destruction of the meridian cities, the rape of beautiful girls, the death of knights and the silence of singers. Night was falling peacefully and neither I, nor the envoy, had the least idea of the future that was about to unfold.

I blushed, opened my mouth and felt an idiotic expression overcome me as I tried to hide my hands behind my back.

Pierre de Castelnau turned to the abbot who no doubt told him that I was the monk with the perfect disposition to plant parsley. He was referring to the absurd superstition that parsley could almost be seen growing when planted by a simpleton. The abbot laughed with acquiescent servitude and they both carried on their way.

I had begun running along the cloisters. I passed the church without stopping.

The murmur of prayers could be heard, for even with the juridical preoccupation, the rules required the uninterrupted reading of the chapters. The one who had started at eight in the evening would only be relieved at dawn. The bell hung in an older tower against which the church had been built. I crossed the doorstep and, like a shadow separated from its body, I climbed the stairs without a sound. When I started the tintinnabulation I was filled with joy. Nothing was premeditated; it was the Tocsin that I rang, the warning signal, in hurried beats, in double beats, in flying beats.

Panic is the emotional element quickest to propagate amongst animals. First I heard the sound of doors slamming on all sides. By the starlight I could see a dozen questioning silhouettes craning their necks.

A stampede erupted in the chapel as all those who had been praying, as well as those with the developed faculty of sleeping in a position akin to prayer, spilled out. They collided with a group of monks who were heading into the chapel to seek refuge. Clamor filled the corridors, the cloisters, and the courtyard. I heard the bursar's voice hollering:

"The treasure, save the treasure!" Laurent with his unstable temperament and predisposition to fits fell to the floor raging. I recognized Friar Robert by his ridiculous rotundness. He'd found, God knows where, a huge cross that he held up with great importance, as if forgiveness for all would be subordinated by his gesture. Suddenly a clear voice rang out, a peremptory voice, that of one who knows.

"It's lord Ussat's soldiers." The lord of Ussat, a man of violence and a convert to the heresy had a long-standing quarrel with Mercus' judicial monks, and had recently threatened to pillage the abbey. He had a habit of keeping his promises. The clanging of weapons followed. Monks were no doubt arming themselves somewhere. Those in the courtyard thought that the soldiers had already broken through the gates.

I carried on ringing the bell. Then, far to the North a bell answered mine, then another to the South and little by little I heard them from all corners of the horizon. They all rang the Tocsin, and their reverberation was infinitely deep, penetrating the valleys and mountains.

I knew which crenellated tower, which church spire they belonged to. One was swinging in the San Salvi tower in Albi, another in the eastern barbican on the ramparts of Carcassonne, another in the church of Saint Nazaire in Béziers. There were some further afield, those in Maguelone, Beaucaire, others rang from sea-stone towers that had shattered Saracen arrows. All of them had an accent of desperation, announcing calamities, resonating the sadness of nations, the death of beauty.

11

Thus the Tocsin that I rang, for no apparent reason, was a kind of signal awakening all the Southern bells, a mysterious universe of bronze whose music was in my heart.

I had no time for astonishment or sadness as I was violently seized as a face almost stuck itself to mine. I breathed in a vile odor that I recognized as belonging to the official bell ringer. He had the appalling habit, either unconsciously or by spite, of breathing his bad breath on you from far too close.

"Why are you ringing? Who ordered you to ring?" He hissed with the indignation of one usurped from his position. I pushed him off with all my strength and no doubt something about me scared him for he stumbled down the stairs screaming.

I followed behind him, listening to the fading bells on the silent rivers, the unknown landscapes. Below the tower a group of monks, who had obviously just interrogated the bell ringer, waited for an explanation. On seeing me they all shouted, wanting to know what danger menaced the abbey.

"Why? What's happened?" They all said, surrounding me.

I began shouting,

"God has left you! God has left you!"

It only took a second for their fear to change into anger and the desire for vengeance. As I ran for my life trying to escape these enraged monks, a hundred voices shouted that brother Dalmas was mad and must be seized. The news of my loss of reason was spread from cell to cell, proclaimed from windows, and one monk who had climbed the steeple to avoid peril, even announced it to the stars, that had begun fading in the lightening sky.

I collided with Brother Robert's belly and grabbing the cross he was carrying, threw it at my pursuers' legs.

12

I sped into a corridor and bolted the door behind me. Sprinting through the deserted dining hall I came out into the kitchen garden. I suddenly remembered there was a ladder at the bottom of the garden leaning against the wall.

I climbed it and let myself fall softly on the odorous body of the vast, indulgent earth. In the distance, in the clover and the vineyards the crickets had started their morning chorus. To the right I saw Sedours' summit, cut like a stencil against the whitening dawn. I knew that by following the Ariège, I would find, not far from here, a fordable part of the river. It would then only be a few steps before I could bury myself in the forest where no one would be able to find me. I started running again. As I ran, I tripped on a hump I had not seen and fell to the ground. My open arms were hugging a burial mound covered in grass, on the top of which stood a stone cross.

My Lord! I found myself pressed into the clay under which Martial rested, as he had wished, without a coffin so that he would all the quicker be taken up by the roots. For a second as I made the effort with my hands and knees to lift myself up, I heard his voice.
He said: "Go, my child, into the forest where you won't hear the resonance of human speech. Learn from the howling wolf, the cracking branches, and the noises of water on river stones. For the living word is born from man's silence. Those who, like you are destined to perpetuate the truth with soaring speeches, have to prepare in solitude for your verbal birth."

Elated by his words I set off again, clear about my mission.

⚜

*Cleric from Fontfroide abbey that the pope sent to suppress the heresy in the south of France. He rapidly became odious by the violence of his repression. Raymond VI, Count of Toulouse was especially the object of his hatred. De Castelnau had undertaken a personal campaign to rid him of his vassals.

13

*The papal envoys were religious bureaucrats. To reinforce their authority they travelled with both lay clothing and a magnificent costume. It was the one who was to become saint Dominique who first had the idea, to beat the Albigensians at their own game, simplicity and poverty, and he made his way barefoot and begging.

*The Albigensian heresy taught that life was sin, in which man is condemned to live repeatedly, through countless reincarnations, until he manages to release himself from desire through absolute disinterest.

II

I lived in the mountains like a wild beast. During the day I'd watch the squirrels jumping from branch to branch, the lizards sliding on the stones and the grasshoppers jumping in the grass, like diurnal stars. In the evening I went down to the farms in the valleys where the women gave me bowls of broth, made from their dog's leftovers. I could hear the men complaining inside the houses and I would catch sight of their angry looks. For in the lands of Foix most had converted to the new heresy and therefore hated all those who wore the robe and tonsure.

Only one, an old man with a goiter, who was the master of a sheepfold belonging to the lords of Lavelanet, befriended me and saw that I got my daily sustenance. My strange destiny was always to interrupt the favorable run of things. One night, I found the goitered old man in front of his door, asleep next to a jar of steaming fresh milk. Most likely a part of the jar was to be mine. I took the jar and emptied the contents on the old man's goiter. He woke and screamed, as if the milk were his own blood. All sorts of rustic creatures appeared from the neighboring stables and I only just had time to escape their pitchforks.

Without knowing it, as if by a magnet, I was drawn to Toulouse and left the mountainous region for that of the plains. It was only mid-August. I picked grapes from the vines. I spent my nights in stables and sometimes, just before dawn I bathed in one of those big stone washing basins, shaped like a Roman tomb, that I found in the middle of a silent village.

I was not happy.

15

My tonsure had disappeared under my growing hair. A beard had sprouted on my chin. An animistic and vigorous force enveloped me. My clothes had become rags. Something unpleasant overcame me that I couldn't exactly place but felt when I ran my hands over my face. I would remember my Platonic lectures and Petrus' promised apparitions with regret, confusing them in my spirit, the philosopher's book and Jesus' presence.

Then one morning, from the top of a hill, I recognized a village near Pamiers I had visited in my childhood. I had accompanied my father who had been asked to repair the church. I went down the slope and headed towards the village. It was Sunday and the people were leaving the church. I saw, from a distance, some peasants considering me with attention. They were talking amongst themselves and I heard someone say:

"It must be that mad monk who escaped from Mercus abbey.
They immediately made movements towards me and I recognized that primal and savage look on a few people's faces that expression one gets when tracking a dangerous animal. My errant life had singularly developed my running skills and in a few minutes I became separated from them by ditches, heath and moorland. I carried on walking a long time knowing the sagacity which man is capable of when pursuing man. I came across a river I thought must be the Ers. I was panting and my body steaming. I rushed to the bank lying down on my stomach to drink.

I realized, to my surprise, that instead of taking the water to my mouth in my hands I was tempted to lap it up in the manner more accustomed to four-legged animals.

When I had satisfied my thirst and was rested, I found myself filled with a well being that had no center and was mixed with an earthly desire. I wanted to sing, to externalize my powers with actions and like a sleeping larva that starts to wake, carnal temptations agitated in the mysteries of my flesh. There was a path that followed the river between tall poplars and leafy hazels. I set off following it.

Frogs that were resting in the grass jumped out in front of me. Despite the love I had always felt for those aquatic beings, I amused myself by squashing them. The squelchy noise they made as they burst under foot, aroused a strange satisfaction within me.

All of a sudden some broom, laurels and low-lying hazel branches obstructed the path I was following. A bit further on, I came to a luminous bank where the Ers widened forming a calm pool, like a sunlit mirror in a sandy golden frame. A woman was lying there, on the sand, protected by the wall of hanging trees surrounding her.

She had just been bathing and must have quickly wrapped herself in a sheet of soft silver-braided linen that enveloped her body. Water droplets glinted on her bare arm and the top of her shoulder, carelessly exposed from the loose veil. The oval of her face was lowered, and thus I could not distinguish her features; her hand was so small that I almost burst into laughter as it rested between her hair, dressed in three plaits. The other hand dabbed the linen veil to dry her body, contouring her lean and perfect outline. The surrounding sun tinged her shadow purple giving the golden sand a reddish hue. The poplar's immobility, the water's silent flight and the beauteous light bathed this woman with a fairy tale mystery.

In spite of her lowered face, I immediately knew who she was, because of her three plaits. Belpech Manor must be standing behind the trees, on the right, leading to its unique octagonal tower. It is there that this beautiful child of Foix, Esclarmonde, came to satisfy her innate love of solitude, with her father's accord. For all good Christians, Esclarmonde's name was synonymous with malediction. She wandered alone in the woods seeking certain dethroned pagan divinities, whose language she spoke and who descended from their mountains at her call. She had no fear of men, for the demon inside her pushed her to give herself to them.

Her father, Roger the count, possessed with a unique love of riches, sometimes came to stay in his Pamiers Mansion, to extort the monks of Saint-Antonin. Insanity!

17

He would entrust Esclarmonde to his aid Roaix, to whom he had lent the little tower of Belpech where he lived alone. Roaix came from a Toulousan family and since childhood, converted her to the Albigensian heresy. It was even said that Nicetas, the man from the Orient, the one they called the cursed pope, had secretly visited Belpech to perform a magical ceremony, whose execrable rite had forevermore chained the young girl to the new church.

This is what I had heard from the gossiping monks of Mercus and in particular from Brother Robert. I wasn't at this point aware that almost everything that is comes out of a fat man's mouth is dictated by evil thoughts. Brother Robert was no exception he was a fat and slanderous man of little soul. He thought he knew it all and when he couldn't bring proof to his tales, he maintained to have been given the knowledge from direct, divine communication. When he spoke of Esclarmonde he crossed himself and pretended to fear the evil spells that surrounded her.

I clearly remember what he thought he had seen. Returning one night to Saint-Antonin abbey, where he had been sent to collect a precious ciborium, he was startled by strange noises. In the middle of this huge avenue of oaks, ending at Saint-Antonin's porch, a naked young woman with a mitre on her head and three golden plaits flowing past her shoulders was playing the lyre. Next to her stood a bearded old man wearing a turban and a Persian or Egyptian costume, he didn't know for sure. Behind them, a long line of forest wolves ceremoniously walked in step, their brazen eyes flickering flames. There were slithering snakes, strange jumping toads and some birds with oddly human expressions on their faces, in spite of their beaks and feathers. Father Robert added that all that had saved him was a host that had remained stuck to the bottom of the ciborium.

I had only given these stories a doubting belief. I had even laughed about it several times with monks more sensible than I, who in truth, were quite numerous in Mercus. Esclarmonde's name kept a mysterious resonance.

18

I only had to pronounce it to evoke images of sin and magic. Here was that witch with the beautiful face, haloed by the legend of her damnation, lying down in front of me on a sandy bed, lit by the mirrors of sunlit water in the voluptuous south of France!

I should have run away out of natural shame. It is a sin to stare at one who's vowed their soul to evil. Fear should have set my teeth chattering. An unknown force heated my blood, which then rushed to my temples. I knew little of women. Before becoming a novice I would sometimes roam the side streets of Toulouse that ran from Saint-Sernin to the ramparts. In the evening the streets were filled with songs and music from those Oriental instruments called darboukas, which are so melancholic even when played for joy. There were both Jewish and Moorish streets. It was in a Moorish one that I lived. I had heard the "love talk" in a ground floor flat. It was furnished only with a sordid mat, a chest for clothes, and an earthenware bowl for ablutions. I heard frolicking behind the wall, the shouts of fighting women and drunken soldiers in the street, punching and shouting that it was their turn.

19

I had retained the memory of a dark voyage on a perdition boat, amongst the stone waves, in an ignominious storm.

Now, memories of guitars flooded back and plaintive songs carried on drunken voices. I breathed a carnal fever. Somewhere a darbouka was playing sadly. It felt like the prescience of a bad deed one is about to accomplish.

I carefully spread the laurel branches and as I crept forward felt a bestial expression invade the features of my face.

The young girl didn't see me. Her stillness stopped me in my tracks. Then she moved her head and it was like an undulation of form. Her milky neck poured down her shoulder and lost itself in the folds of linen like a living ray of flesh.

I surged forward like a blind beast. I tore through the branches and across the sand, throwing myself on my out stretched prey. She was light, ethereal and devoid of strength. I seized her around the waist and set off running straight ahead, stirred by the instinct that pushes the savage beast to go to earth.

I heard a weak moaning and her delicate arms tried to push me off. This movement of her body against mine doubled my bestial fury. I bounded through the bending branches and sweeping leaves. I only slowed for a second to prevent her shock of flowing hair from catching in the bushes. When the path turned away from the river, a little distance in front of me was a mass of dense forest, which stood with its shadows and propitious solitude.

Were a few servants belatedly giving chase to rescue their mistress? Had the villagers, who were chasing me, found my tracks? It seemed to me that cries rang out behind me and that there had been the whistling of an arrow in the air.

Already I breathed the freshness of the tall trees and so close, the dwellings of the wolves' and the birds of prey.

Lowering my head, I saw for the first time the face of the one I had carried off. The half opened mouth let me see the lightning of her teeth. The features were of almost childlike youth, but they expressed none of the bewildered terror I would have expected. My hairy, sweaty face and my manly breath didn't confuse or horrify the young girl under her light linen veil. Whilst running I became struck with astonishment. I leaned further over. Then I perceived in the regular oval of her face a singular geometry.

In the correspondence of her noble eyebrows, in the hair line and the folds of her mouth a superior calculation hid a number that escaped fear and desire. This metaphysical riddle lay in lines of flesh and I felt they were far beyond my intelligence. I searched for the solution in the look she gave me. This look, however, was blue and immense like the avenues one sees in dreams, bordered with hieroglyphic columns, whose undefined perspective end up at a phantom temple. It was a look, devoid as much of hatred as of forgiveness yet icy like the sword of the last Judgement.

A new sensation took hold of me with imperial violence. I was a man on the run, carrying not a woman, but the spirit's tabernacle. I had stolen the saint of saints of an unknown religion. I couldn't measure the mysterious extent of my sacrilege or its consequences in the land of angels and the punishment that would befall me. The spiritual light elected a creature, choosing the most perfect one in which to incarnate and immediately the beast had rushed in to satisfy the primordial law. This symbolic beast was I. I was the height of a crude force. I represented the extremity of materialization. I was contaminated by greedy self-interest. I was a leper with festering sores.

I held in my arms this perfect form and put her on the ground, surprised that I had not been consumed by the contact. She stood like a statue, still piercing me with the cold foil of her eyes.
With both hands together, she crossed her veil over her breasts.

She was translucent. There was nothing but pure light under her veil.

21

She stood in front of the sombre mass of the forest, covered in the splendor in which one imagines the Gods are dressed, somehow estranged to the shape of trees, to the color of the air, to the earth which didn't dirty her feet.

On all sides I heard human voices approaching. I wanted to fall on my knees and cry, but life's instinct was stronger. In a few bounds I reached the forest of high trees and lost myself within.

III

The setting sun made the watchmen's helmets sparkle, like steel lamps on the tops of the barbicans. I saw Toulouse standing before me with its Babylonian gathering of roofs and turrets. I perceived the town squeezed in its circle of reddish ramparts, like a knight in the purple of his jerkin.

I reached the Montolieu gate just as four men started shutting the iron-studded doors. Fearing that the guards were looking out for me, or that I would be taken for one of the bigots, whose entry to the city was forbidden, I slipped in amongst a group of beggars and peasants as they crossed the drawbridge. Since I had long lost the habit of feeling the excitement of the big cities, my steps naturally carried me to the rue de la Pourpointerie where I exalted in its splendor.

Toulouse, in the epoch of its counts, could only be compared with Byzantium or ancient Alexandria. The knights returning from the crusades had brought back oriental fashions and the taste for ostentatious, colorful fabrics. Through Aigues-Mortes and Narbonne came boucrans* from Tripoli; Gerber haïks, ivory and ostrich feathers from the Maghreb. There were boutiques filled with multicolored parrots in cages, dazzling goldfinches on exotic perches and Nile ibises standing on one thin leg. Others had lapis lazuli from Khorazin flowing from metal trunks, whose sides were covered in coral of all nuances. Others so full of musk and aloe that one kept the fragrance in ones clothes for several months, just from passing by in the street. One came across Negroes from Barbary who looked like joyful demons, Moors from Seville or Grenada who wore green silk turbans and Byzantine merchants with cunning eyes.

Behind the litters' muslin, one caught sight of the Toulousan nobility looking like princesses from Baghdad.

The shutters slammed and the lamps were blown out. The folk wished each other good night before shutting themselves in their houses. The magnificence of this dazzling rue de la Pourpointerie was extinguished like the closing of a casket.

I recognized a few familiar silhouettes passing by and some young girls with whom I had once exchanged glances. I lowered my head avoiding their stares.

I turned into rue des Augustin and entered the suburbs. It was whilst I was in the rue des Juives that I noticed I was being followed. A beggar from of the group of people with whom I had intermingled, passing the Montolieu gate, was obstinately marching behind me. I made a big detour by way of the rue des Trois Pilliers to lose him, but the time had already come when, in the central districts, chains were hung at the extremities of the roads. I was going to have to wait until the next day to knock on my father's door.

I headed for Saint-Sernin. In the shadow of the sacred basilica the paving stones on which I would sleep would be like a feather bed to me. It was a soft September night. The church rested on its cruciform nave like a huge stone bird, eternally resting. The five octagonal floors of her tower seemed to throw themselves into the starry sky, and in the superimposed architectural movement, there was an ardor that communicated with my mortal heart. Next to the church, like her brother, the ancient oak of Toulouse spread his branches over the sleep of his thousand birds.

As I wandered across the garden, full of tombs and cypresses, which enrich Saint-Sernin, I heard footsteps and saw a man coming towards me. He was a very ugly old man, whose appearance was just as miserable as my own. I recognized the pigheaded beggar who had been following me since the Montolieu gate.

To many people I have always inspired a spontaneous sympathy. I wasn't particularly surprised to find the old man was one of these.

"I recognized you immediately," he told me. "You are among the believers from the church of Paraclete, the one who has been chosen for the most hefty task. Here you have come faithfully and at the fixed hour. For know this. The times are changing. The antichrist's reign is coming to an end."

It was thus that the heretics spoke of our holy father the Pope Innocent. I wanted to explain to him that, until recently, I was a novice in a monastery of the order of Citeaux, but he wouldn't listen to me. He spoke incoherently, occasionally casting a pitiful look my way.

"Poor child! You are young and you are strong, but your shoulders will bow and your heart will break from all the blood you will cause to be spilled." I thought that the miseries of an errant life had damaged his brain. I told him I was seeking a suitable place to sleep. "Yes, sleep, while you can," he answered me. " It's easier to outrun a raging wolf in the mountains, than escape the actions one is destined to accomplish. We both have our missions: but yours only beginning whilst mine is at an end."

I set out towards the old dwelling of Pierre Maurand so that the shelter of his porch would protect me from the night's dew. I lay on the ground and the old man sat next to me. Suddenly, he pointed his finger at the cross situated on the highest point of Saint-Sernin's bell tower. From there it seemed to pierce the bluish gathering constellations.

"You see that cross," he spoke again. "Before I die I must rip it off the bell tower where I put it myself fifty years ago. I was the hardiest of masons' apprentices. On the day of the inauguration of the bell tower, in front of the Count, in front of the Capitouls* and in front of the bishop of Toulouse, I received the perilous mission to go and plant the cross in the sky the moment the mass was celebrated.

One cannot be afraid of the immense space and the interior funnel that vertigo creates in the soul. Where the fifth floor finished, there were only a few shaky planks above the void.

I climbed with the cross at the end of my uplifted right hand. At the top of the steeple I opened a trapdoor and holding on with one hand, I sunk the cross into the metal groove. Then, full of pride, I looked around. I found myself in the middle of the sky, in a perfect solitude, and the truth of the world appeared to me. There was no basilica under my feet. The murmur of the people in the roads and the reverberation of liturgical singing had no reality.

It was above me that the real basilica was unfolding, beautiful with its transparent stones, its altars and its dreamy Christ. For we only see the appearance, the material double of the ideal reality. I heard singing in the clouds. I saw a celebration! Under the luminous curves of the vaulted ceiling, between the pillars that cleft the sky, a prodigious mass unfolded whose host was the sun. I wanted to throw myself across this divine world. My destiny, unfortunately, was to live and bear many more burdens. From that day on I've had the power to distinguish, in each person's personal atmosphere, the future deeds they must accomplish.

I wanted to chase this lunatic from my presence. He had the kind of inspirational voice that made me think. He started talking about the sadness of the times and the misfortunes about to happen. He put them down to a unique cause. The presence of gold in the world. As gold had penetrated the churches, so God had left them. A golden Christ or a picture or artifact that is even part gold, becomes a symbol of evil, tainted like a pure wine in which one pours a drop of the deadliest poison. The church of Saint-Sernin was full of gold. There was some in her crypts, in her altars' ornaments and in the shrines of her saints. She was no longer worthy of carrying a cross on the steeple of her tower. It was up to the one who had put it there to wrench it off. This heretic's discourses interested me in spite of the blasphemies woven within them.

It was the moment I decided to listen to him that I fell into a deep sleep.

I must have slept a long time. The sound of a trumpet woke me. I immediately thought of death and the trumpet of the last Judgement. It didn't make enough noise to come from an Angel's breath. I realized that the beggar was no longer next to me and that both halves of Pierre Maurand's door were open. Furniture and all sorts of objects were piled around me. They must have been brought there while I slept.

There were oak cabinets, Roman seats, damascene tables, copper lamp stands, silver cups and vases from Pyrenean rocks! Brocade and gold laminated materials, belts and armor made sparkling piles. A marble Goddess on her side was giving me an enigmatic smile.

A tall and slender man stood on the doorstep blowing the trumpet. He stopped and as I got up he came towards me. He had long white hair and an expression of such softness on his face that I didn't recognize him at first. It was the old Capitoul* Pierre Maurand.

I was only a child when a shocked Toulousan had been condemned for heresy. The Papal envoy only let Pierre Maurand live, on the condition that he made a pilgrimage to Jerusalem. In spite of his eighty years he went on foot and embarked at Aigues-Mortes. We had thought that he would never return. I could remember his hardened and irritated face when I saw him being led down the rue du Taur, surrounded by soldiers. It was another man that I now saw, plucked of all passion, like a leafless tree that's still full of sap.

"Take whatever pleases you," he told me. " It's as much yours as mine."

He must have noticed the miserable state of my clothes, for he picked up a robe with a collar and fur cuffs and handed it to me.
Then I noticed behind him a group of whispering servants who seemed dismayed. Their eyes were fixed on the robe.

27

One of them made a movement to fall on his knees before his master. Pierre Maurand stopped him.

Some heads peered out of the windows. I saw shapes coming from the back streets of Saint-Sernin. There were some ruffians and some of those people that one only sees at night amongst the city hovels, whose faces are so astonishingly pale and monstrous. They heckled amongst themselves. I heard someone shouting that there must have been a fire. A young woman with hanging breasts and a crafty smile was looking at my sumptuous robe. She must have thought that I was an important lord for she started simpering around me. Pierre Maurand had randomly picked up a few objects strewn on the ground and tried to distribute them to his servants.

"Take this furniture, take these clothes," he said. "I no longer want any possessions. Take them all!" There was at first a moment of stupor. In the whitening light of the morning, I saw looks of defiance on the scoundrel's faces and grimaces of fear as they formed a circle. The poor always think that generosity hides a trap. Pierre Maurand didn't stop shouting:

"Take it, Take it all!"

As there was something a little bizarre in the accentuation of his voice and the gesticulations of his thin arms, they thought it an act of folly from which they must profit immediately. Suddenly, they rushed forward. I saw arms opening to grab, silhouettes shattering and falling on all fours. The furniture rolled on the paving stones with the noise of chariots. A kind of dwarf was nearly squashed by the canopy bed he was dragging. A man who had thrown a carpet on his head ran away with a candelabrum in each hand. Each one seemed to be stealing what he was being given.

Stupefied, I stood still, in my splendid robe. Pierre Maurand no doubt thought that I was held back by timidity for he put a silk bonnet on my head and then picking up a necklace of precious stones, he threw it around my neck.

At that moment a half-dressed man, who seemed to have been woken by the noise outside, came out of the house crying:

"My God, Oh My God!" I understood that he was the house steward. He questioned the servants, reproaching them for not having warned him, for not having gone to get the magistrates soldiers to disperse the rabble.

"You have no heirs," he told Pierre Maurand severely, "but you will still live a long time. Let us at least save something, for the times when you will be more reasonable."

Pierre Maurand made a quiet sign of refusal. I saw what seemed to be small flames dancing on my chest. It was the stones on the necklace he had given me. I felt a strange burning sentiment where anxiety mixes with delight. It was the first time that I had precious objects in my possession. As if this object communicated with me a fleeting appetite for greater riches, I threw myself down with the girls and vagrants who remained on the paving stones.

I seized a Cordoban leather belt by its diamond buckle and I pulled it towards me. An old woman uttering threats had taken hold of the other end. There I was like a dog pulling a bone towards him into a dead beast's quarry, when I heard Pierre Maurand answer his steward:

"Yes, riches are bad for everyone, even for these miserable folk," and he stretched his hand towards me, in a gesture of pity. "Everyone has to cross it, it's like a test. It's in gold's rot that man finds his purity." Another Albigensian heretic had spoken similar words at the beginning of the night.

"And this? Must one also give them this?"

Like an irresistible argument, the steward placed in front of his masters' eyes an object he had been keeping under his arm.

It was a painting in which a skillful artist had reproduced a woman's face, in the style of the ancient Greeks. Pierre Maurand made a greedy movement to seize the painting and tilted it skyward to get a better look at the image. His slightly mad expression gave way, for one minute, to that sadness without consolation that is found in beauty, lost forever. He lifted this woman's portrait, towards the purple haze of Saint-Sernin, as if to bathe it in eternal light. Then, turning his head, he threw it far away.

"All material attachments distance us from the spirit," he spoke softly, as if to himself, changing his voice. We heard the far off noise of the chains being removed from the roads. The bells started ringing. A line of monks came out of Saint-Sernin and made their way through the cypresses. The older grave stones glowed in golden ivory tones.

I let go of the belt that my hand had continued to grasp. I got up and let the fur cuffed robe fall from my shoulders. I tore off the fire drop necklace and threw it to the ground. All of a sudden I thought that I saw Esclarmonde standing in front of me, as she had stood before me on the edge the Ariège forest. I experienced the same sentiment towards Pierre Maurand as I did for her, that inexplicable and superior presence. Just as it is distressing to be left cold by what is beyond your comprehension, I preferred to stop thinking and strode off towards my father's house.

*Capitouls were the municipal magistrates elected by the people. There were twelve for the city and twelve for the suburbs. They held considerable powers. In the Count's absence they sometimes even declared war without consulting him.

*Boucrans are Genovese woven woolen garments.

*Haïks are Arabian capes, most commonly worn by Moroccan women.

IV

My mother and father were delighted to see me again, but I understood that their joy was tempered by their fear that I might engage in some further senseless act. During my absence, my five-year-old sister, Aude, had returned from Blagnac. She had been in the care of some farmers for the countryside was considered necessary for her fragile health but I didn't pay much attention to her as I had little interest then in children.

When I was suitably dressed my father accompanied me to the Arab baths in the rue Saint-Laurent. They had just been built by the architect Bernard Paraire and were similar to the hammams found in Grenada. He left me at the entrance and headed off towards Saint-Cyprien. He was going to speak to the thugs who had been commissioned by the count of Foix, to find me and bring me back.
He hesitated as he left me, telling me that he would be waiting in front of the main door when I came out. It wasn't the pursuit of the ecclesiastical authorities that he feared, as he had assured me that both the Capitouls and the Count of Toulouse could easily protect me from the Bishop. It was some other danger that he feared for me.

The baths were full of people and the doorway so crowded a child could not squeeze through. I passed women of extraordinary beauty moving as if gliding. Even-though they wore fur dresses their beauty gave them the illusion of having no clothes on. I could not distinguish if they were noble women or those kept by our Lords in the most beautiful houses in town. There were two baths, one for the men and the other for the women, connected by a small stone staircase and a gallery bordered by sculpted arcades.

I was astonished at the familiarity of the people and the topics exchanged. How had morality become so licentious in just a few months? Was I really in the same town where, only a few hours before, Pierre Maurand had distributed his wealth to beggars, because of some mystic love of poverty?

I finished bathing and was compelled by my curiosity to climb the stairs and crouch between the arcades. Within minutes I felt someone next to me and turned to see a young girl smiling at me. I recognized her as the impudent one, whose sarcastic laugh had ricocheted, like the icy droplets of water dripping off me as I climbed out of the bath. At the time I thought that she was mocking my gaucherie, for God, with irreproachable care, had fashioned my body with little attention. Instead of being half naked under a light veil and a silver net to hold back her wet hair, she now wore a fuchsia dress over a silver-lamé tunic and baggy trousers. She had wrapped her head in a massive amaranthine turban, which accentuated the violet color of her eyes. It made me think that she was a Saracen or one of the captives the Crusaders had brought back from Jerusalem.

"Follow me," she said laughing, "but when we're in the street, pretend you don't know me."

If I'd not been so confused her foreign accent would have made me laugh. I was not sure if she was being serious so I gave an embarrassed reply that my father was waiting for me in the rue Saint-Laurent. This seemed to double her mischief, as she grabbed my sleeve and with a movement of her head and a wink of her eye signaled me to follow her. We passed the women's pool and my embarrassment grew in front of the spectacle of general nakedness. She noticed my unease and as a joke put her little hand over my eyes. She led me to an exit that opened onto a side street. There a jovial matron and a bronzed beauty carrying a huge package overflowing with scarves and bathing linen met us. We set off towards the square where a crowd was gathering around a monk who was standing on a stool, sermonizing. His face was menacing. I overheard some words as he pointed his finger at the baths.

"They revel in the rot of their own bodies... They are like beasts eager to mate... They have lost their honor, the very foundation of purity."

I recognized the monk condemning the baths. It was Petrus. I was amused at remembering the little care he took of his own personal hygiene and the friendly reproaches I had made on the subject. I would have waited to talk to him, but had to keep up with the imp in the amaranthine turban who was already turning at the end of the road.

We walked to the Bazacle district where the roads are lined with high stonewalls, hiding antique gardens. Suddenly the three women disappeared and I came to an open door that led into a garden. Large sculpted box trees framed a mosaic water feature and yew trees like the high thoughts behind women's smiles, towered above the hyacinth and jasmine borders. The sand in the paths was mixed with gold dust. Invisible birds sang amongst giant roses. A Moorish house stood at the bottom of the garden and in between the spindly columns one might have read the Koran, above the filigree arcades.

As I lingered, astounded at the novelty of what I was seeing, I heard the stranger's fresh laughter. I recognized her charming and foreign accent. She was angry because someone had forgotten to put nutmeg into the hyssop and honey wine and because the snow sorbets weren't arriving quickly enough. Then all of a sudden, she appeared in amongst the roses and asked me why I stood like a simpleton, yawning in the middle of the garden.

I was staggered by her impudence and charm. Oriental women are certainly different from those in Toulouse, I thought. She told me her name was Sezelia, but thought it ridiculous, as the barbaric Christians gave it to her on arrival in Marseilles. Some Venetian had stolen her from an island, whose name I couldn't understand and had sold her in the Provence. It was there that she was baptized and introduced to mass for the first time.

33

I understood by the lightning in her eyes that her conversion was only skin deep and that experience must have taught her that religion is the one thing that cannot be spoken of with honesty. She had been bought by an older man from Genoa, who had then brought her to Toulouse. The crystal of her laughter shattered and took on the resonance of hatred when she spoke of him. She remembered her country with longing, where the arts were loved and she told me she considered the Christians semi-barbaric, driven purely by their appetite for opulence.

She made me drink and eat so frequently that I became dizzy. Then she played the darbouka and wept. After that she laughed louder than before and took off some of her clothes to dance. The afternoon faded. I lay on animal pelts. The perfumes of the hyacinth and the roses from the garden mingled with those of a resin that she occasionally threw into a bowl of burning embers. I felt strangely drunk. Even though I had shaved that morning and was as clean as a clerk, Sezelia said that I was as hairy as a peasant. As she brought her cheek close to mine, she pulled back squealing that I had scratched her. I was savoring the beauty of the moment. I had the vague apprehension of being the victim of an enchantment.

While Sezelia was lying next to me, chattering away, a name hit me. It was the man from Genoa who had brought her to this Arabian home in an attempt to try to keep her happy and prevent her from leaving. His name was Foulque and he was the new bishop of Toulouse, recently ratified by the Pope in a scandalous election. He was famous in Provence and the Languedoc for his immoderate taste in women and the appalling poetry he wrote for them. He had only known disappointments in love because of his ugliness and his foul habits. After years in a dissolute life, he started an ecclesiastical career as it was the one in which riches came quickest. She told me he had developed a bitter and active hatred for the race whose daughters refused him and that he was one of those rare men capable of causing pain in a disinterested manner.
"Bishop! That's the title with which he endlessly prides himself," said Sezelia shrugging her shoulders.

I didn't have time to reflect on the trouble I was in and my demeanor must have darkened at the name of Foulque because Sezelia tried to reassure me.

"He won't come today. He's celebrating a mass because they are going to fell that famous tree next to Saint-Sernin." I jumped up, grabbing and shaking her.

"Are you sure?   The Saint-Sernin tree?"

She answered that she was sure and that it was happening now, commenting that the people of Toulouse must be deprived of common sense, to attach such importance to the life or death of a tree.

It was a drama that had been going on for over a year. A thousand year old oak, full of countless birds, stood in front of Saint-Sernin's main door with its branches engulfing and bathing it in shadow. It was older than the church and even older than the city itself. It had watched over the Romans, the Goths and the Saracens. It was said that a nightingale came there to sing, but only on the night of Saint-Jean. Toulouse's soul lived in the depth of its roots and on the wings of its birds. The choirs complained that in the spring, during vespers, their canticles could not be heard over the noise of the sparrows and swallows.

So the Prior of Saint-Sernin, an old and sallow man, embittered by a bad liver, had decided to chop the tree down. He had the right, the tree being within the boundaries of his monastery. The councilors had opposed it but count Raymond had washed his hands of it. As a result it was put to the justice of the new bishop whose election was nearing and meanwhile the people's love of the tree was doing nothing but growing.

I deeply shared this love. Still holding Sezelia by the top of her lamé tunic, I got her to tell me everything that she knew. Foulque had given orders that the tree must be cut down by dusk.

35

He had told her the day before that the people of Toulouse were no better Christians than she, a Saracen and he aimed to humiliate them and the pagan cult that surrounded the tree.

Sezelia's tunic had torn in my hands, baring one breast that spilled like a living flower from a vase. I turned and ran towards the gate. She gave me an imperative order not to leave but I took no notice and waved adieu.

Quick as a flash she took a dagger out of a chest and chased me through the garden trying to stab me. Her tunic was completely ripped.

She stood half naked between the cypresses, as if between two dark guardians, she looked like a golden, violet-eyed statue. She screamed insults at me in an unknown language and as she threw herself at me I had to twist her wrist. She fell to the ground, a bronze and defeated fury, bathing in her disheveled hair. I saw her, as I looked back, throwing a fistful of sand and rose petals at me. Once outside I began running towards Saint-Sernin. I felt light and full of life.

I ran past people standing in their doorways and others running with me still discussing the unfolding events. A fat man shouted for his wife to come and lace up his breastplate. A lance that had been thrown out of a window nearly landed on my head. In the rue Saint-Rome, I mingled with a group that was heading in the same direction and I caught up on the fresh news.

The Capitouls had just seen count Raymond. After remaining silent in their presence for a long time, he tossed a coin in the air saying that if it was tails he would stop the bishop from felling the oak. As it was heads, his face lit up and he said he could do no more. Arnaud Bernard wanted to get the town's militia to defend the oak but the other Capitouls were too scared. Around Saint-Sernin the soldiers had blocked the streets. In the crowd I shouted that we had to keep moving forward.

I realized that my voice had an unusual timbre, reverberating far away. The people looked at me with surprise and amusement when I said that a few soldiers could not contain the people of Toulouse. This explanation shot through the square and was heard by the protestors. A human wave lifted and carried me to the first row, right in front of the sergeant-at-arms. I felt the unpleasant chill of his breastplate, similar to that of a snake.

I pushed the man and his icy breastplate over with such force that the crowd cheered with joy, then following my example, surged onto the square. It was at the precise minute that the first axe blow struck the ancient tree. Bishop Foulque had thought he would compel some peace over the town by celebrating a solemn mass and the hymns and organ rang out simultaneously.

They had requisitioned the executioner and his aides to cut down the tree. I saw their vile figures fill with fear. The monks from Saint-Sernin, who had stood in two rows, scattered like leaves. The disorder was indescribable. The soldiers gathered in little groups and sheltered behind their shields. The cavalry ran amok, striking at random and leaving a moaning trail behind them. Several of the younger men had recognized me and had gathered round. I heard them shouting:

"Dalmas! It's Dalmas!" We formed a human chain around the tree, each swearing to die rather than back down.

Then, between the Saint-Raymond hospital and the monastery there appeared a mass of cavalry, like a metal wall. These horsemen swung their lances into the crowd as if they were scything wheat. Another iron wall was coming up the rue du Taur and was about to smash into the square.
The Capitoul Arnaud Gilbert, whiter than the white washed walls of his palace, arms spread wide like an obese Christ, begged us to abandon the oak's defense. I saw, on the right, the executioners' red jerkins behind the silver of their breastplates.

I understood that the tree was condemned. So, with this brilliant voice that God had just given me, I shouted:

"Let's Burn it!"

A few seconds later, someone put some burning straw in my hands, and I heard voices shouting:

"Yes! Burn the tree!"

The oak had some deep cavities full of vegetation made flammable by a long drought. No sooner had my torch fallen into one of these, than a tall crackling flame rose to meet the higher branches of dead wood. A great glow trembled in the square, glittering off the armour, and terrifying the gaping figures at the windows.

No doubt in the church, the flames in the windows must have given off a sudden cataclysmic light and the choirs must have believed they were at the point of elevation. Either to conjure the peril, or to satisfy his old troubadour's theatrical taste, bishop Foulque stopped celebrating the Mass. He crossed the nave and standing under the church's portal, full of arrogance in his sacerdotal garments, he held out a host to the people.

With an immense beating of wings, the ten thousand birds that had made their homes in the oak's foliage rose together, like a cloud, tinted purple by the fire.

While the tree blazed and the birds rose and the bishop lifted the body of Christ, I saw everybody's eyes being drawn high up, on the other side. I looked up and at the extremity of the bell tower, a man hung on to the glowing steeple. His feet weren't resting on anything and as one could not see the steeple, he looked as if he were standing in space, with a cross on his head. There was a massive, singular sigh from all those anxiously watching. The man's arm lifted, seized the cross and threw it into the void. Everyone, for a fraction of a second, saw the man make a step to climb higher, to fly into the sky. He fell bouncing off the tower's levels and landed near a lateral door on a gravestone. A horrific howl followed. As I ran off, I passed next to the man. The skull had burst but the face was recognizable.

He had an ecstatic glow in the death of his eyes. I thought I saw the reflection of his phantom basilica, with its flame-less candles and silent organs that he had told me about last night, towards which he had gone.

I lost myself in the crowd. I walked for a long time at random, pushing myself to find peace. I felt guilty for forgetting my father and for the sin into which I had dived. Tears ran down my face when I thought of the burnt oak and Saint-Sernin who had lost her cross.

V

As the months passed I found my friends again and realized that a great change had come over them. An element of hatred had introduced itself into their souls. Each one had suffered some injustice or another. The monk Petrus had taken up his cantankerous habits again and become increasingly fanatical.

"Have you seen Jesus?" He asked me with severity, as one might ask when something out of the ordinary happens. When I answered "no" he swore at me and told me that it must be due to the heretical perfume that emanated from my being.

My friend Samuel Manassès was increasingly worried and agitated. He lived with the presentiment of misfortune, which, according to him, would strike him and his family. He was so thin and pale that the kids screamed "Ghoul!" when he passed through the suburbs. He helped his father healing the sick and he read Plato. He dreamed of traveling to the Orient to find the Jewish philosopher Maïmonide, sure that he would learn life's wisdom, the hidden secret behind the visible form.

Long before it had reached its climax, this terrible deed I was about to commit had silently begun to germinate in the depths of my soul. For such a deed does not occur without reason. It is like a plant, first a seed and then roots, then a stem that creeps slowly towards the light of realization.

I don't know where God paints his crazy and terrible images or when exactly that sketch was drafted.

Without a doubt it was in the period when I was still on the run from the ecclesiastical authorities. For a while I would only go out at nightfall and my father would accompany me and bring me back to the house when the chains were put up in the streets. I was wandering along the ramparts early one morning when I saw a group of Templar Knights riding under the Villeneuve gate. Amidst their ranks I thought I recognized Pierre de Castelnau's thin silhouette under a monk's robe, which he only wore for ceremonies. The envoy had no doubt been seeking the count's approval on his latest warrants. He wore neither sword nor lance and only had one servant behind him. I caught a fleeting glimpse of his pallid blue eyes, parchment face and two red cheeks brought on by the perpetual fury in which he lived. Then his coat, like a wing, brushed past me and something dark rose within me, sprouting the seed that had lain dormant in my fallow soul.

To my great surprise I saw the procession go past the gallows and head towards the cemetery, where the sanctimonious hypocrites and plague victims were buried. Finding myself in the middle of a gathering crowd, I noticed that one of the graves had been freshly opened. I recognized the jovial face of Tancrede the bishop's executioner. He was clearing armfuls of flowers aside with his feet while his helpers were pulling a coffin out of the earth. It was the spot where Marie the Clothier had been interred a year ago.

She was nicknamed 'the enlightened one' by the people of Toulouse and had passed from life as a saint. All day she had ironed jerkins in her father's little shop in the rue Saint-Rome, murmuring prayers. Sometimes she used to put down her iron to welcome a spirit invisible to all, which she had spotted in the street, or she would announce a future event that never failed to happen.

My mother who placed great store in her eccentricities had brought me to her. I remembered her icy hand on my forehead and the tremor of fear that shook her when she touched me. Under Pierre Maurand's influence she had converted to the Albigensian heresy.

42

Her last prophesy had spread the furthest, announcing that an evil spirit would manifest in Toulouse through three detestable creatures: a man who would wear a mitre, a man who would wear red and another who would be covered in iron.

Bishop Foulque had been singled out as the first, the envoy Pierre de Castlenau as the second. We feared the appearance of the third. Marie the Clothier died aged twenty-five. She had asked to be buried in the plague victim's cemetery. A huge crowd had accompanied her, singing canticles. Now her coffin was shattered by the executioner's pick. Pope Innocent* had ordained that the bodies of heretics didn't deserve an earthly rest, as their souls were condemned to eternal suffering. The judgment had been passed only the day before and Marie the Clothier's ashes were to be thrown to the wind. It's not ashes that one finds in a coffin where a body has lain for a year. Rumours spread that when the coffin was opened the sweet smell of sanctity emanated from within, like the gentle fragrance of lilies and rosebay. Apparently, all the assembled saw Marie with her eyes closed, her incorruptible face still bearing the same calm expression that it had the day she died.

However, let me assure you that I was in the first row of onlookers. The coffin was upright when the lid came off. I saw only a blackened mummy whose absence of expression, and whose teeth, singularly long and apparent, was a vision of horror. I could see nothing coherent left of her body beneath the rotting grave clothes. Pierre de Castlenau unrolled a parchment and began to read the condemnation of the ecclesiastical tribunal to her grinning, fleshless face.

An old man, miserably dressed, pulled me by the arm. I recognized him as Pierre Maurand. He dragged me away from the burial area as the executioner descended on what little still remained of the hapless heretic, tearing her shriveled cadaver asunder and gleefully strewing the pieces every which way, literally scattering her to the four winds. Pierre Maurand seemed neither indignant nor saddened. Only later did I understand what he tried to tell me:

"As long as the body lives, it draws the spirit by its attraction. Happy are those whose rapid dissolution allows the soul to fly away, to the higher regions where one is no longer separated by form! It's possible that Marie was still held back on earth, by the link of a memory, an image, maybe the love for her iron. The executioner's pick has just liberated her forever."

⚜

On the eve of Good Friday, I was due to accompany my friend Samuel Manassès to a reunion of notable Jews, where he was going to represent his father, who had been called out to a patient in Saint-Cyprien. I waited for him where the reunion was happening, pacing to and fro in front of the rabbi's door. When he came out, I noticed he was even paler than usual. I asked him why.

An old custom maintained that on Good Friday a Jew would present himself at the doors of Saint-Etienne cathedral during Mass. He had to knock three times on the door. A priest would open the door and ask him his name. He would answer:
"I am so and so from the race of those who crucified Jesus." The priest would then slap him and the people assembled in the square followed the Jew home heckling him.

Thanks to the enlightened authority of the Counts of Toulouse this custom was no longer strictly followed. The priest lightly touched the Jew's cheek and the crowd made no further efforts to harass him. On the eve of Good Friday, the members of the Jewish community gathered at the Rabbi's and pulled out of a hat the one who would have to go and knock on Saint-Etienne's door.

"It's my father who has to do it," Manassès told me, with trembling lips. I answered him that I saw no reason for distress. "My father has none of the faults common to man and I often think that God has made him a model of perfection. Nevertheless, he does ever so rarely let himself get carried away by his pride!

44

Aware of it he is then immediately repentant. I think he will be mortally humiliated to have to go through with this mission and I'm suffering for the unmerited pain he will endure."

Isaac Manses had returned when we got back to his house. We had agreed that Samuel would read certain passages from the Maïmonide manuscript he had recently received. Whilst taking the manuscript from the chest where it lived, the old doctor asked who amongst his fellows had been ascribed the task at the rabbi's. I heard Samuel reply that it was Lévy the moneychanger in the rue des Nobles. Then in a calmed voice, he read the pages of a higher philosophy, of which I understood not a single iota, but unreservedly admired it to make him happy.

The following morning I went to place Saint-Etienne in time for the Mass. There was an unusually large crowd. I found out the reason for this from the people who had come to watch the novelty of what was about to unfold before them. Pierre de Castlenau no longer wanted a priest to dirty his hand on Good Friday by touching a Jew. The slap was a chastisement that now belonged to the executioner.

I jumped onto the fountain's bowl to see, what was going on at the church door. The door opened slowly and it framed the violet cape and black hat by which one recognized the Jewish notables. The cape however seemed too big, the hat too low on his head. This silhouette was very fragile and suddenly the large, joyful face of the executioner dominated it. I saw him raise his iron fist and then it fell like a heavy hammer upon the Jew who stumbled to the ground.

When he got up I saw that it was my friend Samuel Manassès. The waxy whiteness of his face was stained with blood as he stood wavering. I noticed behind him in the stone corridor, the Christians were all kneeling under the arches of the main nave. The candles sparkled like souls in pain and the Christ on the altar seemed further away than one of those ghosts, glimpsed in the darkest perspectives of one's dreams.

The door closed behind Samuel and in front of him the ebbing crowd made a space. Never in living memory, had a Toulousan crowd shown hatred toward Jews. In the presence of this limp and bleeding young man, a hostile murmur ran through the mob that suddenly bristled with clenched fists.

My unfortunate friend didn't need to make it across the terrible void, which separated him from the wall of furious men. He looked around on all sides as if to find some support, an escape from the violent universe into which he had so suddenly been propelled. Then he fell to the ground like a cedar tree whose roots had been abruptly and irrevocably cut way, his spirit departing him.

The image that haunted me came into focus for the first time at Samuel's burial. Jews could only be buried after sundown and their cemetery was in a far off corner of Saint-Cyprien. Night was falling as the procession followed the Garonne and its wharves. Four young men carried the coffin where Isaac Manassès had insisted on placing Maïmonide's incomprehensible manuscript on his son's chest. I was the only Christian and I walked at the back.

Just then Pierre de Castlenau on horseback rode past me. I felt the breath of his coat and I saw him in the dusky shadows place himself in front of the procession and arrogantly precede it. I didn't fully comprehend why the horse's hooves seemed to make no noise on the flagstones or why no one else was astonished by the envoy's inconceivable impudence. I rushed forward and overtook the procession to seize the silent rider's bridle and to pull him out of the way of the dead one's road. I found him nowhere. As a door was open near the bridge, I thought he must have disappeared into it. Then I caught sight of him again and quickly retraced my steps, a little surprised to find he was now following the procession and not preceding it. Under their violet capes and their hats' shade, the Jews seemed completely oblivious to the rider's presence. Their eyes followed me in consternation however, asking themselves what had come over this Christian, the dead one's friend, to run to and fro, gesticulating without reason.

*In 1206, Pope Innocent III had excommunicated Faenza Abbey because it had refused to unearth a heretic.

VI

My father had his heart set on finding me a brilliant position, and in due course he succeeded. One morning he made me dress in my best clothes announcing that we were expected at the Narbonnais castle. He had to present me to the count of Toulouse, who would do something for me, as thanks for the services my father had rendered.

I was totally speechless. Even though I knew that the count Raymond was a man gifted with the common touch, it was neither his importance nor his great personality that impressed me. I was moved to be so close to the most famous man in Christendom for his goodwill. I naively believed that such virtues could manifest themselves in a physical form. I would not have been surprised, when I found myself in the presence of the count, if I had seen a halo glimmering around his head.

When we were introduced, he was sat like a schoolboy in front of a long marble table where his coat of arms, a golden cross on a black key, was represented in mosaic. He was drinking some white wine that had been brought from Guyenne. Without acknowledging my greetings and neglecting all forms of welcome, he declared that the wine was a bit sweet for his taste and that he was very keen for us to try it. He had some goblets brought for us. He was only satisfied when my father and I had declared that indeed the wine was too sweet. He rubbed his hands together and held me in his friendly wolfish gaze, then he tapped me on the shoulder and burst into laughter, saying:

"You're the one who rang the tocsin in Mercus Abbey, the day the..." He didn't mention the envoy's name.

"You're the kind of brave boy that I need. I'll take you as my squire. You'll start today. I like prompt decisions." His incapacity to make decisions was legendary and almost a sickness. He forced himself to make quick decisions for the smaller issues, thus persuading himself he was a man of resolution.

"Here is Thibaut who will teach you your job." He pointed out the squire who was pouring the wine. He looked like a sly lout, as do so many of our compatriots.

"You will drink very dry wine, from Comminges!" I must have remained associated with a viticultural pleasantry in his mind, for he often joked about it with me in passing.

"What about those poor folk from Guyenne! Hey? Poor sods drinking that sweet wine!"

The count of Toulouse had his magistrate, his cavalry and his infantry in the fortress of the Narbonnais castle. He lived in the rue des Nobles, in a recently built house surrounded by an enormous garden. This house was both legendary and mysterious.

Many beautiful Toulousan women had come looking for him after the curfew. It was said that the King of Aragon, to gain his friendship, had presented him with some Arab captives of marvelous beauty, and that he had a harem just like the King's. One heard singing at night, and one saw light glowing under the trees. Although married five times, the count Raymond kept some love for all his wives, even those he had repudiated, even those who were dead. He cried when Jeanne of England was mentioned because this queen had been so jealous, that she surely could not have gone to heaven. He sent messages to the countess Beatrix who, on his orders mind you, had shut herself in one of Béziers' cloisters. Each liaison, even the briefest, whether with a noble lady or a poor girl, procured him further worries and grief. He would then comfort himself amongst his bizarre animals, assembled in the garden of the rue des Nobles.

49

It was there that Thibaut lead me. He told me that even though I was a newcomer, I had my Lord's full trust, because I had been responsible for the incidents at Mercus and at Saint-Sernin and that I had lit the oak. Thibaut was a taciturn soul, but he knew how to listen and with a few tales I quickly inspired his admiration. He, in turn, filled in my education in the bearing of weapons, taught me the science of armour and how one catches and releases falcons.

I saw the count Raymond every day and he seemed increasingly worried. His little eyes only found an expression of joy in the midst of fluttering wings, when he passed in front of his aviary. The peacocks turned around him, a blue and yellow parrot landed on his shoulder. The swan he had tamed and called "The Twenty-fifth Capitoul" followed him snapping its beak.

"Do you know, he told me one day, that the Albigensian heretics forbid themselves to kill any animal, even a fly? It's because they profess this respect for living creatures that I protect and love them." A dove had come to land on his hand and he lifted it towards the sun.

"Look how God has majestically shaded this plumage, how he makes it pass from white through metal grey and on to a blue that one can't find in any sky. Surely to spill blood is the greatest of sins." I knew that the count of Toulouse had stopped going hunting the previous year. He carried on, without addressing me directly:

"The heretics are right on many points. But what of the Pope's infallibility?" He looked at me and a smile brightened up his face. "There is however one thing about them that I don't understand… No, I cannot understand that perfection is found in chastity."

I wasn't to see him smile again for a long time.

It was that very evening that the rumor spread through Toulouse that count Raymond had just been excommunicated.

The ceremony happened in Saint-Etienne cathedral but only in the presence of a few members of the clergy. It was said that when the envoy had thrown the candle to the ground, and trod on it with his feet, the bottom of his robes had caught fire. No one could be found to carry, as in accordance to the custom, an open coffin to the excommunicated one's door. The envoy and the bishop, fearing the indignation of the people of Toulouse, had been forced to renounce the custom.

We found out at the same time that the envoy had left Toulouse and was on his way to Rome. This departure did little to attenuate the sentiment of his occult presence around me. In fact, the further away he got, the more incensed I became and the more count Raymond's features became fixed in a ghostly expression.

In Toulouse at the beginning of this century, excommunication wasn't as bad a thing as it is today. For many people, the church was synonymous with debauchery and simony. These rumors were not without basis, for since the time of the first Christians, the mysteries of the faith had been lost. Error had taken hold of the clergy and like a poison slowly ravages an organism, it had changed the living flesh into rot. Wealth and power had replaced the desire for poverty. Satan lived in the cathedrals, flowed in the baptismal waters, condensed into the bread of the Eucharist. The preachers officiated in his name. Far away, Rome was like a Babel that enthroned, under a doomed cross, a stone hearted Antichrist.

The first day, the Count refused to see anyone, he hung out with his birds and Thibaut and I. We frequently heard him speaking to his favorite swan, as if were the only advisor capable of useful council. The second day he summoned his high-constable, his magistrate and the Capitoul Arnaud Bernard, renowned for his wisdom and bravery. They stayed a long time shut in together. Then he gave Thibaut the order to prepare his weapons and his fastest horse. We knew that all the soldiers from the Narbonnais castle were alert and ready to leave. In the hallway of his house, balancing his belt in his right hand, the Count paced to and fro.

51

He spoke to me directly:

"If henceforth I refused to heed the Pope's orders, if I sent the envoy's head back to Rome, sealed in a box bearing my coat of arms, wouldn't the whole of the Midi be behind me? It's Arnaud Bernard's advice and he's right: But why do his words carry such vehemence? Who knows! Who knows! Perhaps, in spite of the years, he still hasn't forgotten that story about his wife."

Arnaud Bernard's wife, now old, was said to have not only loved the Count in her youth, but also to have told him so.

The following day, early in the morning, we sped along the road to Carcassonne. The Count was resolved to kidnap the envoy and keep him as a hostage until the excommunication was lifted. He only took a cavalry of fifty, but a small army, under the high-constable's orders, would join them if the envoy sought refuge in Montpellier or some other fortified abbey.

As Carcassonne's towers appeared before us, the Count suddenly halted. His expression had cleared. A messenger approached in great haste from Toulouse's direction. The army was not needed. The high-constable had to return with his soldiers.

"There's only one way to act," repeated the Count, "conciliation, promises and subterfuge."

It would be better to catch up with the envoy before he left the Count's estates. We slept in Carcassonne, and then left first thing. We found out in Béziers that he had stopped there for a day to confer with the bishop of the town. Maybe he was considering renewing the excommunication ceremony in all the cathedrals of the Midi. In Montpellier, he had left the town a couple of hours before and had also had a long meeting with the bishop. My horse, quicker than the others had carried me forward. I had the sensation of realizing a dream, pursuing an obsession that my brain had created a long time ago.

Finally, arriving at Saint-Gilles on the banks of the Rhône*, we were told that the envoy had just entered the abbey to spend the night.

Saint-Gilles was one of the Count of Toulouse's personal fiefs where there was a castle and soldiers. For a long time, however, the abbey had rebelled against him, claiming to answer only to the Pope.

"What if I used this as an excuse not to leave a stone standing in that cursed dwelling," said the Count and he pointed to the walls that straddled the hillock, tall as the walls of a fortress. The following morning, as soon as the sun rose, he presented himself alone, bareheaded and on foot, at the abbey's door. He humbly asked to see the envoy. The envoy answered that the foot of one excommunicated by Rome could not touch an abbey's stone. He gave an order for the Count to wait for him at the castle, where he would come to see him.

"I'll meet him with my helmet and sword in my hand," he told us. "We'll see!" He put his armour on and laid his naked sword before him. The hours passed without the envoy coming to the castle. The count had only hastily eaten a few mouthfuls. He was still shattered by the long journey on horseback. He called for Thibaut and I, so that we might unlace his breastplate and bring him something to drink.

"Take some goblets for yourselves," he added. We had barely poured the wine from Arles when a bell rang out, doors slammed and without even hearing the scraping of his sandals, the envoy stood before the Count.

A Papal envoy had the right to enter anywhere without being announced. By courtesy he rarely used the privilege. He had a monk's robe on that he only very rarely wore. An envoy had the authorization to wear anything from lay clothing to the most glorious costumes that would outshine even the greatest Lord's pomp.

We were used to seeing Pierre de Castlenau under his scarlet hood and his crimson Dalmatia but now he seemed very small and almost insignificant.

He remained silent, looking at the naked sword on the table, the bottle and the three goblets that betrayed the Count's familiarity with us common folk. There was a crushing contempt in his immobility and the stillness of his gaze.

The Count gave us an imperial signal to leave.

Neither Thibaut nor I have ever known what was really spoken between the two men. From what the Count said later to his familiars, he spoke haughtily to the envoy and it was this attitude that ruptured the meeting. It is more probable though, that he repeatedly threatened and then begged him without result. After quite a while, we saw the monk's silent silhouette descend the castle steps and head towards the abbey. I followed him with my eyes. He straightened his little torso and I understood by the way he half turned his head that he feared the arrival, of a crossbow's bolt between his shoulder blades.

No noise came from the room where the Count was staying. When night fell Thibaut and I decided to light a candle and enter. The bottle had been overturned and its contents spilt on the stone floor. The counts head was leaning forward and maybe to find some well being in the cool metal, his forehead touched the sword's blade. When he rose we noticed that he was crying. He immediately blew out the candle hoping that we wouldn't notice his tears. He then asked us in a deep voice to leave him until tomorrow. Shutting the door, we heard him murmur:

"I'm a lost man! Forever lost!

Thibaut and I left the castle and went to the balustrade built above the Rhône, which dominates the port. The wind made the masts and galley's sails moan lightly. I distinguished the river on one side. The extending gloom of the Hermitage lagoons created mists and mirages where the evening light mirrored on the piles of salt. On the other side stood the ramparts. Pilgrims, recognizable by the cross they wore on their chest, were heading towards the town and they stared at us as they passed. It seemed to me that I had already seen everything there was to see and that the events that were about to happen, had already been drawn up somewhere, right down to the finest details. I suddenly said to Thibaut:

"I understood a while ago, without a doubt, when the envoy was looking at the wine and goblets on the table, that Marie the Clothier had prophesied correctly. We have just seen a living incarnation of evil." Thibaut simply lowered his head. I continued: "I've often asked myself how men can support the evils of injustice without rising against them."

"It's because they are afraid," he answered. "Everyone is cowardly. Everyone fears for their own precious lives." Then I began laughing uncontrollably and I was conscious that my laughter was ringing so loudly and that the returning echoes gave my mirth a bizarre and immense inflection.

"I'm not scared for my life." I cackled into the void.

That minute, the deed that I was about to accomplish came out and held itself, like a living phantom between my companion and I. Thibaut saw it with as much clarity as one sees a man standing in front of you. As I strode off towards the castle Thibaut followed, asking me what I was going to do. I didn't answer but he stuck to me. I was acting as if in a dream. I went to the squires' hall, which at this hour was empty, and quickly armed myself. Thibaut did the same even though I told him several times that he'd better go to the refectory, as it was time for dinner and he wouldn't get served if he was late.

He didn't listen following me to the stables. He mounted his horse and galloped after me.

I headed towards the abbey with the confused intention of knocking on the door, overpowering the porter, and entering by one way or another. I'd got to within a hundred meters of the entrance when Thibaut grabbed my arm and forced me to stop. We'd just seen, by the light of the stars, that the door was wide open. A lantern lit up their armour and a group of riders were slowly leaving. They did not speak between them, their weapons didn't touch and it was obvious silence had been ordered.

"That's him," Thibaut told me, pointing out the one who came out last.

The envoy's escort, apart from a few valets, was composed of about twenty men, all Roman and belonging to the Pope's personal guard, but they were not heading in our direction. They took a little path on the left that ran along the Rhône. We followed them. We didn't have long to wonder where they might be heading. A few hundred meters away there was a hostel that the people of Beaucaire shared with a disreputable inn. The group stopped and we watched them all dismount. The envoy, fearing some nocturnal endeavor by the Count, had decided to cross the Rhône above Saint-Gilles.

"Night brings wisdom," Thibaut said, staring at me.

We presented ourselves at the inn an hour later when we saw the glows in the windows go out. First we had to haggle. We didn't want to use our titles as the count of Toulouse's squires. Unfortunately Thibaut was from Beaucaire and the innkeeper recognized him.

"The whole inn has been rented by the abbey of Saint-Gilles," this man explained. "There are Italians everywhere, even in the stables, with the horses. My own footmen are going to sleep in the barn next to the pigs."

Nevertheless there were some pilgrims who had been waiting for a week for their embarkation to Jerusalem. They had occupied the attic and, if necessary, we could join them and shelter there for the night. The heat was stifling and a human odor poisoned the air. Thibaut was most preoccupied to find out where they might have hidden those "Ladies of leisure" that one found in all the inns of the Provence and which gave this one its reputation.

"The ladies must be hiding in the neighboring barns," he told me several times, with regret in his voice.

We kept on our breeches and chain mail tunics and lay in silence for a long time. Unable to sleep, we decided to light the candle, but the tallow had softened and it only gave off a vague glimmer. We only saw, without joy, our lurid expressions so we blew it out. Every now and then a sleeping pilgrim shouted or grunted and scratched at the vermin on his body. It seemed to me that beneath us there was a felted step pacing to and fro. Late in the night, the moon rose, it gilded the wheat, and lit the sleepers as if they were corpses.

With the rhythm of silent footsteps, thoughts came to me. What lurked in the soul of this man who knew no sleep? He was a monk who had devoted himself from his youth to things of the spirit.

In Fontfroide abbey he had earned the reputation of being one of the brotherhoods most studious and pious adherents. He had read and meditated upon all the manuscripts, discussed Plato and maybe even Maïmonide. It was because of his great intelligence that the Pope had chosen him, not because of his compassion. He had lived in Rome and it's there that the evil spirit had taken hold of him in the form of arrogance. Once kind, he had become violent to the point of sometimes losing his reason. He loved jewels and dressed magnificently. Condemnations brought him a visible joy. He didn't hide his thoughts with bishop Foulque, that half the inhabitants of Toulouse should be burnt as heretics.

What was the sum of one man's life? Did it deserve so much reflection? He, the envoy with all the great Lords and the Pope brought death to men without remorse, under the pretext of justice. At the time of the first crusade, when they had taken Jerusalem, the crusaders commanded by a Saint, Godefroy de Bouillon, deliberated for three days on whether they should massacre the seventy thousand inhabitants of the town. After three days deliberation, they decided to exterminate them. Raymond Saint-Gilles, Count of Toulouse, was the only one to protest and he saved those he could, helped by the people of Toulouse, my brothers. So, it must be that human life has no price and there are other invisible forces beyond our mortal ken that determine its true value and the consequences of our deeds in this earthly plane.

I can vividly remember every second of that night. Hatred wasn't in my heart. I was an instrument of God, a cog in a massive machine. For good as for evil, God gave the same power of growth, allowing for creation as well as destruction. For right as for wrong he had the same love, it seemed to make no difference.

Injustice was the stronger, as it could not be limited by any interior law. What would happen if justice lacked courage? Yes, it was obvious that God wanted evil. He protected the bad, giving them material power; incomprehensibly he even went so far as to place the crown of divine intelligence on their foreheads. Then at a chosen hour, he thwarted them with an unexpected action from an obscure man. God set about his work in the spiritual realm, just as he weaves his patterns in the material world. First he deposits a seed. This seed, whether fecundated by the earths sap, or by thought's essences, always grows slowly. I found the proof in the substance of my memories. The action had seeded itself in me like a plant. I was the depository of a divine seed that was about to realize itself in the physical world. It meant nothing to me that I would have to inevitably pay for it with my life. I was consumed with a sacrificial desire, marked out as surely as if I bore an invisible brand upon my chest.

At some point I ended up by falling asleep. I woke with a jump and although it seemed as if a century had passed, daybreak was not upon us. Thibaut was up and trying to see out through the skylight. I dimly heard the neighing of a horse.

"Are they going?" I asked him in a whisper and he nodded his head.

I leapt to my feet in one motion. At the same time we saw a fat spider seeking a way out on the edge of the skylight. Thibaut went to squash it. I grabbed his arm. He looked at me with surprise.

"Have you changed your mind?" He asked me. I shook my head and in silence took off my chain-mail tunic. Again he considered me without understanding. I explained that I did not intend to escape. Without the chain mail those that would strike me could kill me quicker. Then he picked up my helmet and held it out to me, insisting that I drop the visor over my face.

"One never knows what might happen. If you escape, it would be better that no one recognized you as one of the Count's squires!"

As we were leaving the attic, I saw a redheaded man sitting down, stroking his beard and watching me wide eyed. With my helmet shut and my cloth shirt barely tucked under my belt, I realized that I must look like something out of a nightmare. A footman was pushing the stable door closed when we arrived. Thibaut said that we were lucky to find our horses. I answered him shrugging my shoulders saying that I would reach heaven or hell just as easily on foot as on horseback. With meticulous care he took off the pennons from our pikes that were attached to the saddles.

A sloping path led to the area where the boats docked. It was lined with bull-rushes and tamarinds. The river was calmer than usual. Dogs were barking in the distance. The newborn light was so delicious it almost made us weep. The majority of the riders had dismounted and one of them spoke to a boatman who with bare legs was pulling his boat to shore.

A few paces away I recognized Pierre de Castelnau's solitary silhouette. He was seated upright on his horse, his head inclined forward and for a moment he seemed so vulnerable, that if my heart had been accessible to pity, it would have broken at the sight.

Holding my lance under my arm, I pushed my horse towards him. Human life is even more fragile than what one might believe. Almost without resistance, the weapon sank into the soft matter of his flesh and penetrated deep within.

I'd often heard it said, that to be certain of bringing death, one must twist the blade and rip it out and I was determined to do so. The man's face that I had just struck suddenly turned into a frightened child's mask and I heard him cry:

"Mother!" He reeled in his saddle. I let go of the weapon and watched as a scarlet stain of blood appeared between his lips. I had the impression of staying there forever, in the middle of a universe held hostage by death's enchantment.

The moment the envoy fell from his horse a clamor rose on all sides. I saw the Italians' faces turned towards me with looks of horror, but it was as if I was detached from time and space. I noticed how different the shapes of their faces were from my compatriots and I regretted not having enough time to study these differences of race. My thoughts like an unruly machine jumped at random, setting themselves strange problems. "Why is there only one amongst them who has a full beard? Never will so many horses be able to embark on such narrow ships!"

Events never happen as one imagines they might. The people escorting the envoy must have thought they were being attacked. The majority, taken by panic, got back on their horses to escape. A few of them circled around the envoy.

I noticed that Thibaut had ridden up beside me and that we were suddenly almost alone on the sand.

The rising sun stretched our shadows out of proportion, like giants' shadows. I had promised not to defend myself once I had struck. Once free of the thoughts that immobilized me, I drew my sword. Feeling my bare chest, I quickly asked Thibaut to lend me the round shield that was hanging from his saddle. It reflected the globe of the sun, like a reddened gold coin at the bottom of a fountain.

He held it out to me, but no one attacked us. So he led me behind a few tamarinds towards the road to Beaucaire. We joined it but without hurrying, stupefied at not having to fight. After a few paces we took off at a gallop. We looked back frequently, but no one gave chase.

"We got away with that one," Thibaut said. "I counted about twenty-five of them. We can hide at my parents house in Beaucaire." He glowed with an air of profound satisfaction. He was slipping his sword back into its scabbard when I rode in front of him waving my arms. I wanted to go back and fight. I was taken by a mad desire for death.

"We're cowards to run away. Let's kill them all." Thibaut had great trouble calming me down and making me go on. A little before Beaucaire I suddenly got off my horse. The morning air had cooled my blood. I couldn't stand it any longer. I pleaded with my companion to abandon me, to let me go to sleep under a birch tree that was spreading its shadow on the roadside. He pointed out a little tower that stuck out above the ramparts, swearing that it was his Uncle's house and that we had nearly arrived. In the end I gave in and decided to follow him.

I've never felt any remorse. For a few nights I heard a muffled voice crying, "Mother!" and I saw that dismal face with blood running between livid lips.

Immediately I would think of my friend Marcayrou, who had been hung as a heretic and I remembered the big bird of prey that had pecked out his eyes.

I had uselessly thrown stones at it, as I prowled under the gibbets to see what was left of my friend. I would think about the young Rosamonde Colomies, the armourer's daughter, who had been blessed with the gift of expressing herself with such eloquence. She must have been all of twenty and she was both wise and beautiful. The envoy had heard that she had talked about chastity amongst the heretics. I imagined the underground prison of Narbonnais castle that held, without sexual segregation, the hardest criminals, the insane, and even the lepers escaped from the Lazar houses. They lived in that tenebrous hole, in the most abject conditions, continually fighting the rats.

There were other less awful prisons in Toulouse, but I believe the envoy had personally seen to it that Rosamonde Colomies had been thrown into this living purgatory saying that the more beautiful the criminal, the greater the risk for God, and hence the need for more exemplary chastisement.

I've felt remorse for many of the things I did in the span of my long life; against men defending themselves in battle, against innocent beasts who looked at me sadly when I struck them, but for the deed I committed that night I have never felt the slightest remorse.

* Saint-Gilles was, at the beginning of the XIII'th century, a port on the Rhône where the pilgrims embarked for Jerusalem.

* There was an enormous abbey and the town counted at least thirty thousand inhabitants. Due to the Rhône's changing course, it is now a village surrounded by land.

Part Two

I

I left Thibaut in Beaucaire and went back to Toulouse, alone and by the roads less traveled. I found my parents sick with worry. Lord Elzéar d'Aubrays, the count's marshal, had been to my house several times inquiring upon my return. It had come out in the talk that he'd had with my father that I should already have been back in Toulouse. The count Raymond had said that I had left Saint-Gilles the tenth of January. However it was the morning of the fifteenth that I struck Pierre de Castelnau. I immediately understood that the count had purposefully given a false date for my departure, thereby averting any suspicion that might have fallen on me and blaming the envoy's escort for his death. Having rather limited political views, I couldn't yet imagine what great interest he had in avoiding any of his entourage being suspected of the envoy's murder. I was choked with tears by his show of fatherly caring.

When I saw the marshal at the Narbonnais castle, he didn't ask me if the count had given me some message to deliver. He showed no surprise at the length of my journey, but examined me with extreme curiosity, without manifesting the bad mood and arrogance that had made him feared by all. A rumor was running that he had joined the heresy, but that it had not softened his character. As I was about to leave him he told me that I was a brave servant to the count and then he suddenly asked me a strange question:

"How can you see in the dark?"

Taken aback, I answered that I didn't have cat's eyes and if it was a black and moon-less night, it was as impossible for me to find my way as for anyone. He bit his lip and dismissed me, repeating that I was a brave servant and after all, that was enough.

I became aware that Pierre de Castelnau's death had brought great joy to the whole city. To my surprise though I'd heard some people expressing fears over his assassination, saying serious consequences were inevitable. As much as people held forth on the character of the murderer, no one suspected me. Because of this need to speak that every human has and that I possessed in abundance, I was obliged to make a huge personal effort to refrain from telling the truth. I confided in no one, not even my father. However I did not yet know that truth, more fluid than water, permeates without the need for words.

It seemed to me, that around this time, because of my actions, certain hidden forces had been suddenly set free. I started eating and drinking more. My voice, already well developed, gained even more resonance. Secretly I began to look for quarrels. I was overcome by a sensual desire for women that I had never experienced before. I went to a hammam in the rue Saint-Laurent and saw Sezelia again, for events have a tendency to reproduce themselves in the same way. She welcomed me with the same happiness and invited me to go and see her, which I did. Mysteriously an image re-emerged in my soul. With an extraordinary clarity I saw in her the face of Esclarmonde de Foix, just as she had appeared to me, just as I had contemplated her on the sand of that little beach on the banks of the Ers. She stood in the background of my dreams, and vaguely lit them, like an image of the goddess Minerva, on top of a city of ghosts and larvae. I started no longer believing she was human, but ethereal and of ultra-terrestrial essence. Also, when I heard that her father, the count de Foix had married her to the viscount de Gimoez, I was overcome by a sentimental aching and a sadness I couldn't understand. This sadness grew the day I met Esclarmonde de Foix, viscountess de Gimoez.

Night had fallen and I was heading back to my father's house at the end of the rue du Taur. A little old man approached me, with a face wrinkled like a long fallen apple. All his wrinkles started moving and he turned towards me, offering me a friendly, welcoming smile. He took hold of the sleeve of my doublet and asked:

"How do you see in the dark?" At the time I made no connection between this question and the Marshal who had interrogated me in an identical fashion. I've believed a few crazy things. The night was very clear. I lifted my head and answered with a straight face.

"I see because I am illuminated by the light." I was going to say "of the stars", I've no idea why, but I said: "by the light from on high." This answer caused much jubilation in the little old man. He took me with familiarity by the arm.

"I knew it! I knew it! But why have you never come to us? This evening you must come with me. There are many who wish to meet you." I followed him without resistance, I've always followed the principle that you must obey destiny when it gives you a sign. My train of thought in this period was such that at first I thought I was dealing with one of the many Bacchanalian characters in the city. Morality had dropped and people were talking about nocturnal gatherings where folk belonging to the finest families got together with the sole aim of partaking in an orgy. The beautiful Guillemette, widow to the lord of Lezat, as well as other high born ladies attended, they said, with veiled faces, under the pretext of reconstituting pagan festivals and satisfying their own lascivious leanings. Supposedly the poet Pierre Raymond frequently attended these conclaves and the austere Capitoul Arnaud Bernard had promised a ten Melgorien penny reward to anyone who could inform his police force of any of the infernal locations. As we made our way, my companion's discourses threw me into some doubt.

"If one is slapped on the one cheek, should one offer the other as Christ said? You've just shown, my child, in an explosive way, that all Albigensians are not ready to die without defending themselves. Many of our brothers reckon that you've committed a great sin. I want to tell you personally that I don't share their opinion." He was leaning over me, with an air of confidence. When we reached the Dalbade neighborhood, he spoke again:

"The higher levels are difficult for us to reach. Everything depends, obviously, on how many lives we have behind us. Did you know that Saint Paul incarnated through thirty two lives before passing into our Father's care?" I answered that I wasn't aware of the exact number and asked him how he had come to know of it.

"The number is precise," he said, contenting himself with his affirmation. "You are young! What a long race you have left to run! What lives you have to live!" I couldn't work out from his voice whether he was sorry for me or in wonder. His words seemed to be a poor preparation for the scenes of pleasure that were coursing through my imagination.

"Here it is" said my companion showing me the Roaix's ancient homestead. I suddenly realized that the old man was none other than Frederic de Roaix, the famous Capitoul's brother. Several people, two or three of them women, were entering the half-open door the moment we arrived. I saw, by their baleful faces and those stripy skirts that are so popular with the prostitutes, that they were girls from the suburbs. I even recognized one of them who'd got the nickname 'Scrawny', because of her terrible wretchedness. She was a miserable girl, always shoddy and in a bad mood. I'd had several arguments with her.

I began sniggering, judging her and imagining the scene in which I was about to find myself.

Having crossed a courtyard, I was pushed into a big, bare hall that was lit with flaming torches.

66

Folk belonging to all classes were gathered and spoke in low voices. A certain religious gravitas emanated from everyone's attitude. I understood at once that this was a gathering with a very different character from the one I had imagined. As I was standing, taking in the scene, a side door opened and much to my astonishment I saw Esclarmonde de Foix.

She wore a black dress with buttons up the front and a violet shawl over her shoulders. No gold or gem sparkled on her person, apart from her hair that was held back by a shining sapphire encrusted in a silver band. This marvelous blue-green stone placed in he middle of her immaculate forehead, had something supernatural about it. I was hit by the sadness that emanated from this young woman. She looked straight ahead, a little above the peoples' heads', as if she were following a series of events unfolding in an invisible universe.

The old man who had led me here split the crowd, approached and spoke to her in a low but familiar tone. He pointed his finger in my direction and no doubt said something of little interest, as she seemed to take no notice.

My features were etched with such surprise that a young man standing near me, who seemed both naive and intelligent, leaned on my shoulder with goodwill and said:

"I see you are a neophyte. The lady Esclarmonde is, for the believers, the symbol of pure spirit incarnated in matter. You must have heard about Helene de Simon?" As I remained silent he nudged me on the shoulder. So I made him understand, with a gesture, that I barely knew this Helene. My eyes remained fixed on Esclarmonde, who had now taken a seat in the middle of the assembly.

"We are human," the young man started again, " we need our conceptions to take root in the human world. As you think about the Holy-Ghost coming down to earth, think of Esclarmonde de Fix's beauty."

"What are you talking about? I don't need the Holy-Ghost to think about it." I brashly answered this idiot.

But the Holy Ghost obviously played a major part in this evening. I realized that everyone here was thinking solely of the Holy Ghost. Wishing it would enter them. Various orators had their say, one after another, announcing its accession. The Holy Ghost from the Orient blew on the world to enrich it. Toulouse was the chosen earthly capital. Everyone should receive the Holy Ghost in the secret tabernacle, found in the very depths of our soul.

I was bathed by the mystery of these incomprehensible words. Around me the faces were beaming. I could sense a happy, joyful and pure exaltation lifting like the smoke above a bonfire. But I felt as if a thick, damp bark enclosed my soul and prevented it from catching aflame. There was something mysterious and ineffable in the air that made me want to cry.

"What is this Holy-Ghost?" I asked my neighbor, for I felt that it was not the same one that was written about in the Christian mysteries. But before he had the chance to answer me, I got up adding:

"I also want to give my opinion on the Holy-Ghost," for I've never been able to listen to someone speak without also having my say. The young man gently took me by the arm, smiling.

"Words have several meanings, depending on one's level of understanding. For me, the Holy-Ghost is the force that helps one tear away from the material plain, the current that flows back to the divine source." I shrugged my shoulders and started towards the little stage where the orators were speaking. Then I saw Esclarmonde de Foix get up. She walked forward, her hands lightly stretched in front of her. Frederic de Roaix was pushing a woman towards her and I recognized the miserable wretch of a creature that was called 'Scrawny'. She was trembling and almost prostrated.

Esclarmonde made her rise in one motion and took her head in her hands. Stupefied I saw long ivory fingers in the middle of a hedgerow of hair and the one I compared to Minerva placed her lips on the girl's* forehead. A long murmuring followed. Several groups had formed, animated in lively discussion. An old man raised his voice to explain the beauty and the attraction of death and how much every one should desire it.   A bald, clean-shaven man had started walking strangely around the room defining a circle, walking faster and faster.

"What's up with him?" I asked my neighbor.

"He's doing this because only the circular movement is perfect. He wants to imitate the pure spirits who only move in circles." The old man's voice had become imperative.

"Rip yourselves away from this life which is evil, escape from this rot so that you might approach the true essence of being."

"That's going too far," shouted a sensible looking individual with bowlegs and a square head. "Otherwise the one who killed Pierre de Castelnau must have turned him into a happy man." He said from the back of the crowd

That name unchained a world of contradictions. They all started talking. Everyone was passionate about the subject. I noticed that Frederic de Roaix was going to and fro, whispering hither and thither, and pointing me out.

"He's one of the count of Toulouse's squires! He's one of us." I stood as straight as I could. For a minute I felt an extreme arrogance. It's true; I'd not understood anything that had been said about the Holy Ghost, but never mind! I had a different role. I was a man of action, the heretics' liberator.

Slowly an empty space formed around me.   Then my eyes met Esclarmonde's. She was looking straight at me.

She was looking at the man who had killed Pierre de Castelnau. It must have been impossible for her to recognize the wild creature that had grabbed her and ran off with her in his arms. Her look pierced me like an iron lance, sharper than the one I had used to kill the envoy. All of a sudden I read in her eyes, as in a book painted with living images, the horror of my act, the disgust she surely felt for my uncouth and bloody soul. Then she turned and disappeared through the door by whence she had entered.

I looked about myself, searching for a friendly face but the young man who was standing beside me, stepped briskly away. Heads turned, avoiding my gaze. What I had taken for admiration was only contemptuous curiosity. Only old Roaix, who I spotted from the back with open arms, still seemed to be on my side.

"We need such men! They are despicable, yes! But so what!"

I made a move towards the door. I found myself face to face with 'Scrawny' and was humiliated to feel how much a friendly word from her would have been precious to me. This girl's wrinkles were full of ecstasy and she held her forehead up, as if one had placed the Holy Sacrament on it and she was scared to let it fall.

Maybe my doublet rubbed her dress? I must have made a vague gesture towards her. A wild hysterical scream rang out and she leapt backwards, tightening the creases of her dress, looking to run away, as if from the most repugnant dirt.

The strangeness of the scream froze everyone. Seeing me in front of her, many thought that it was because of something I'd said or done. I heard wrathful words. A tall man, who looked like a knight, declared in a loud voice that if I had to be punished, he only needed telling and he would carry out the deed. With his open arms he parted the crowd around him and walked towards me.

I took a step forward, working out a way to jump at his throat in an attempt to take him down.

I felt an insupportable suffering that I hoped I might escape with my own violent game. Then an unknown force, similar to a sob, but a sob with a life of its own, was agitating my chest, rising then regressing only to rise again. So I was already in the world of evil! My vanity tore in two like a dress and it seemed to me that I was naked, naked and miserable like the first creature contemplating the first sunset in a universe laden with shadows. I fell to my knees shouting:

"I ask for forgiveness from all. I did wrong, I can only do wrong and I don't understand good. Enlighten me, those of you who know! Don't leave me in the shadows. Hold out some helpful hands, my brothers!" With my forehead I touched the stones where Esclarmonde had stood. I breathed the dust that her dress had lifted as she passed.

Much later that night, a sergeant-at-arms who was carrying a lantern at the end of his spear gruffly asked me why I was staring so intently at the Garonne's flowing waters.

I could have answered that I was a squire to the count of Toulouse, the son of the famous Rochemaure and that he should go on his way without worrying about me. But I told him very politely that having made the acquaintance of good and pure men; I would not rest before having discovered the veritable nature of the Holy Ghost.

⚜

*Albigensians practiced absolute fraternity. Many young men from noble families married humble prostitutes as a symbol of their love of all of humanity.

II

Count Raymond returned to Toulouse and I was the first person that he wished to see. He sent for me from the Eagle tower, situated on the Narbonnais castle's Northern quadrant. He was dressed for war and as I went to kneel before him, he took my hands. They were limp and a little humid. He squeezed them for a long time, fixing me with his eyes that were always a little gummed up. We stayed like this for a few minutes and in this silence were spoken the words which couldn't be pronounced. He started pacing to and fro and I noticed a soldierly air about him, a spirited gait.

"How do you think Pope Innocent welcomed the news of his dead envoy... He held his jaw in his hand for more than a quarter of an hour, and then he invoked Saint Jacques de Compostelle... And how do you think Saint Jacques de Compostelle inspired him... He's mounting a crusade against the South of France! Against me, grandson of Raymond Saint-Gilles who conquered Jerusalem. But he has no doubt that his crusaders will come and spread themselves like dust in front of the wall of metal and stone that I will raise in front of them. My nephew Trencavel is not over the moon at the thought of fighting the Northern cavalries. He's bringing five hundred Aragonese riders that he'll pay with his own fortune, and as for me..."

The Count's projects were immense. He had written to the king of England. He had sent messages to his vassals in Albi, Carbine and Provence. Toulouse's armourers worked without a break, forging swords and lances. Under the Capitoul Arnold Bernard, the people labored night and day repairing the ramparts and raising new towers. New militias were organized.

An order had been given to keep the shops shut until ten a.m. in order to give time to those practicing the arts of war. Amidst this chaos the women seemed more beautiful. The businesses boomed and the streets were full of joy. For the perspective of an on-coming war is like a wine, which makes you, drunk for life.

Nearly every evening I went to the public ball that was held in the fields next to the Montolieu gates. But there reigned such a warlike mentality that it became fashionable to dance with a sword on the hip. The dancing lost its appeal due to the fighting over all the torn dresses. At the beginning I'd found pleasure in being the center of every-one's attention. But soon it began to bother me. The young men around made a point of not quarreling with me. I saw apprehension on many faces and when I danced a vacuum immediately formed around me.

I got great pleasure out of visiting the poets. Pierre Raymond took me along to the recitals where people read their poetry. They went on for most of the night. Guilhem de Figures, the grocer was there with those "ladies" that so often accompanied him. He couldn't go an hour without a drink; so one of the "ladies" slipped him a bottle of wine from the folds of her skirt when the crowd acclaimed the beauty of his poems. Gerard le Roux was there too, famous for his feminine success and his big feet. I even saw Pierre Vidal*. He looked sad and old but he was preceded by such an enthusiastic reputation, that he only had to open his mouth and show his wobbly teeth for everyone to be in awe.

It was me however who got the biggest laugh, the night I read the first poem of my own composition. Surely the sadness of the subject did nothing to motivate the laughter, so I made up my mind from that day onward to avoid the company of poets.

I had somewhat forgotten Sezelia. When I did go and see her, instead of the reproaches I was waiting for, she asked me suddenly.

"When are you leaving Toulouse?"

I answered that I was beholden to the count Raymond and he had no plans for leaving at the moment.

"You must leave Toulouse, as soon as possible."
"But why?"
"The town is going to be totally destroyed, from top to bottom."

I thought first of all that this was one of those follies quite common with womenfolk. But she insisted over and over, she even suggested going together to the Orient under the pretext of a pilgrimage. I started getting worried. I urged her to tell me what had led her to believe in Toulouse's destruction. That city, whose origin is lost, obscured by time and which is most probably immortal like the planet herself. She finished by admitting that she had gleaned the information from Foulque, the bishop of Toulouse. She told me that he hated the city because of the heresy of its inhabitants. Little by little, he had identified the heresy with the houses and monuments. The corruption had infiltrated the very stones; it ran in the rivers, took shelter in the shadows on the dark side of the streets. He dreamed of an exemplary punishment. Most of all, the churches were doomed. They would be demolished stone by stone. The bells would loose their curved form and become ingots once more. As I was rendered speechless by this abominable project, she gave me some more details. Bishop Foulque had written to the Pope to explain the need to destroy the heretical capital. The bishops of Foix, Albi and Béziers supported him. Like the rest, messengers, who came from the North every day, kept him in touch. The crusade against the Midi had been preached with the same passion as the crusade against the Infidels. An enormous army coming from France and Germany was going to meet in Lyon and invade Occitania.

I decided to bring these matters to my master, the count of Toulouse. But I never got the chance. When I presented myself in front of him the following day, he threw me a severe look and clearly unnerved, he told me that he was leaving for Saint-Gilles that very day. He would take other squires than Thibaut and myself, for we were not the sort one could safely take to such a place.

He left Toulouse in a hurry and with barely an escort.

⁕

Returning a month later, I saw him in the knights' hall the day he arrived at Narbonnais castle. He looked disheveled but despite his haggard expression I understood by the way he winked at me in passing, that he still cared about me. That evening, Thibaut and I received orders to be ready to accompany our master.

"We must be armed," Thibaut told me. "Apparently we have an appointment at the Chapter-house." The count of Toulouse had summoned the Capitouls together. It was customary for him to go to the Chapter house, to mark the authority of the town's magistrates over their lord.

As we rode out of the rue des Nobles, we were joined by a figure who wore a sword, belted over a black cassock and looked as much like a soldier as a clergyman. I readied myself to push him off when the count turned and said:

"This is brother Laurent Guillaume. He, unfortunately, is bound to me." We found out a little later that he was one of pope Innocent's men.

The Capitoul's house was behind Saint-Sernin, nestled amidst the suburbs. It was an ancient roman edifice, quite possibly a former temple that had been renovated. On the facade, twelve columns resembled immobile stone magistrates. The surrounding roads were cluttered with the consuls' horses. The count was already climbing the steps of the threshold when I saw the one he had referred to as Laurent Guillaume crossing himself several times. He approached me with a crafty expression and told me in a hushed voice.

"God gave me the good sense to perceive the emanation of pagan or heretical thoughts. This is a place where Idols have been worshiped!"

75

I rather bluntly suggested that he should stay by the door with the servants and horses in order to avoid such painful perceptions. I must have mistaken the rank he held for he didn't answer but walked calmly behind me, lowering his eyes.

The twenty-four Capitouls, from both the city and the suburbs were already sitting in their sculpted wooden stalls. I noticed an unaccustomed rigidity in their backs. Arnaud Bernard, with his square jaw, resembled a geometric enigma. A few of them wore sumptuous robes. Bernard de Colomiès was making the rings on his twitching fingers positively sparkle. Raymond Astre trembled under layers of fur. I saw eyes shining from cunning negotiation, the big farmers' strong shoulders, the money handlers' long and twisted hands, the furrowed brows and pallid faces of Albigensian asceticism's myriad practitioners. The intermittent torch flames, aggravated by a draft, gave bright light followed by deep shadow. At the far end of the hall a wooden Christ, covered in mould from the moisture in the air, looked as if it was actively decomposing.

I'd just taken a seat behind a balustrade, which stood opposite the stricken Christ, next to a few scribes and servants, when an angry rumor arose. Foulque the bishop had just entered the chamber. Theatrically he crossed the room and went to sit in the chair opposite the count. The Capitouls at first dumb with shock, had begun to get to their feet, talking agitatedly amongst themselves. Several made ready to leave. Others facing the count were saying things I couldn't hear. In the end, Arnaud Bernard's voice dominated the hubbub:

"The members of the Chapter would like to know who summoned the bishop to the reunion?" Embarrassed, the count got up and answered. It was he. Did all decisions not have to be approved by God's representative? He had just reconciled himself with the church. The excommunication that weighed on him had been lifted and he sincerely hoped that all the people of Toulouse would rejoice.

76

The account of what had taken place in the cathedral at Saint-Gilles had been circulating since the morning. Milon, the pope's legate, had flogged the count of Toulouse stripped naked to the waist.

He had then been led down the dark side of the basilica and made to prostrate himself in front of the remains of Pierre de Castelnau. I had heard the rumors and knew only too well that the people of Toulouse were not rejoicing about the humiliation of their lord. Etienne Cerabordes, the market gardener and Pons Barbadal the wine merchant, sharing the same thought, spat simultaneously to express their disgust.

"Isn't Toulouse the most powerful city in the world?" Shouted Pierre Guitard. Count Raymond, pale and resigned, tried to explain himself.

"I believed myself obliged to bow before pope Innocent's wish." Outrage interrupted him.
"And why?"
"Why believe the Antichrist?"
"It's the pope who should explain himself here and on his knees."

Bishop Foulque got up. His face was covered in a mask of hypocritical sadness but he had trouble hiding his detestable joy. Squeezing his chest in his hands, he beckoned his children to return to the church's fold. He knew how the heretical snake devoured them. For a long time he had been forced to stand idly by and watch as this symbolic serpent bit at the hearts of the people of Toulouse but now he, Foulque, would crush the snake's head beneath his foot.

"Can you remember Barrel des Baux's foot," shouted Arnaud d'Escalquens, a fat and happy man who had the faculty of expressing his thoughts as soon as they were conceived. Indeed it was well known that before entering the order, Foulque had courted Azaleas de Marseilles and after a boorish attempt at seduction, she had been forced to have her husband kick him out. Once more Arnaud Bernard's voice rang out, high and vibrant.

77

The quadrilateral of this bearded figure was turned towards the count.

"What have you consented to?"
I saw my master lower his head, and then with great effort, he began talking quickly.

He explained that the army gathered at Lyon was enormous and even now awaited new reinforcements. All the Northern barons were there. Eludes, the duke of Bourgogne, Hervey, the count of Never and the count of Bar, all cruel and unscrupulous men. They were led by Simon de Montfort, an English adventurer from the Leicester family, chosen as leader because of his absolute absence of pity. Some faithful folk from Provence had travelled up the Rhône and returned, giving my master recent intelligence on the army's intentions. It was uniting purely for pillage. The crusaders were speaking of Béziers, Carcassonne and Toulouse just as Godefroy de Bouillon's companions had spoken about Jerusalem. It was the wealth of these cities and the beauty of its women that fanned their desire. My good master had thought he was doing his duty in sacrificing his arrogance in order to save them.

"What about our soldiers and our ramparts?" Shouted Arnaud Bernard who still had dust in his hair from cutting stones on the towers where he was overseeing the reparations. The richest amongst the Capitouls were pondering, sharing the same fears at the thought of the pillage. Then bishop Foulque began to speak. How God had been merciful to enlighten count Raymond's heart! He had allowed him to repent. The count of Toulouse repented for the scandalous leniency he had, up to now shown the heretics. Once again he had become a beloved child of the Holy Church. And what had the Holy Church asked in penance for this repentance? Almost nothing! For she was magnanimous towards sinners. The Count of Toulouse would give six strongholds to the crusaders. He would give full power to a religious tribunal to bring justice back to the land. He would take part in the crusade with his own cavalry.

A long silence followed. Everyone thought they must have heard wrong. All of a sudden an enormous peal of laughter was heard. It was Arnaud d'Escalquens who was pretending to take the bishop's discourse as a joke.

"So will the count of Toulouse have to lead his enemies across his own estates!"

Suddenly everyone exploded in protestation. Thus their ancient right to render justice was abolished! An ecclesiastical justice would no longer be justice. If the Northern crusaders came to Toulouse, they would find the drawbridges lifted and the people of Toulouse on the ramparts, even if the count was amongst them!

"Only heretics need fear the crusade", said Foulque calmly, "and there are some among you now who tremble...."

"Well, what about it? What if there were heretics among us?" said Pierre de Roaix turning towards the bishop, his marble face framed in a crown of white hair.

"They will die! Even if they are Capitouls like you. The ecclesiastical justice does not recognize the inviolability of the Capitouls."

I thought that several people were going to throw themselves on the bishop. I felt a hand grab my arm. Next to me, Laurent Guillaume had drawn his sword.

"The time has come," he said, "to set upon these sad Toulousans." I told him that he was in the presence of the most illustrious people in the city and if he didn't sheath his sword, he would have to deal with me. I heard the count's tired voice, still trying in vain to legitimise his conduct. He had thought about it having measured the present forces. In the event of conflict, defeat was inevitable. It was true, he was sacrificing the Albigensians, but Toulouse would be spared.

"It would be better if Toulouse perished!"
"We'll never give up the Albigensians!"
"We'll keep the bishops and clergy as hostages!"

Foulque had left his chair and was retreating towards the back of the hall where the few men who made up his personal guard were standing. When he was amongst them, he lifted his open hands above his head, as if he was pushing an invisible image into space.

"Toulouse will be like Sodom and Gomorra! Horses will use your beds as troughs! The soldiers in their camps will raffle your wives and daughters, with chains around their necks. Colomies the jeweler, we'll gut your chests of pearls! Astre the cold blooded, the road workers will put on your furs and you will run naked in the fields to keep warm! Arnaud Bernard, builder of walls, we'll plough the land where you built those barbicans! Then you can all invoke your invisible pope!"

A wooden pole was arrested in mid-air by a lance as it was about to land on the bishop's head. The Capitouls fists clenched, lunged toward him as one. Foulque retreated to the door, surrounded by his guards' weapons. The wind blowing stronger bent the torches flames to such an extent that the hall was plunged into momentary darkness. Then we heard:

"In the name of the father, the son and the holy-ghost, I curse the heretical people of Toulouse!" When the torches' palpitations had finished, the bishop had vanished.

The Capitouls were already raging. Pierre Cerabordes and Pons Barbadal were shouting that they were good Christians and they laughed in the face of the Albigensian heresy. Others pleaded with the count to arrest the bishop, split away from the pope and unite the armies against the Northern barons. The count with arms crossed and eyes fixed tapped the floor with his feet, insisting that his decision was irrevocable.

But I understood by a particularity in his eyes that he was prey to uncertainty and was internally imagining the consequences of changing his mind.

Maybe there was time enough. If at this moment the count of Toulouse had cried out: "Men of my land, be with me, let us unite against our common enemy, even if this enemy is the pope in Rome!" maybe Occitania would have been saved. Obscure witness to this scene, I was tempted to jump in the middle of the hall to persuade the count to come back on himself, for the people of Toulouse to unite with their lord.

But what value has the words of a young squire? Beside myself only one man seemed to understand the importance of this moment and, measured the possibility of bringing the count back, by some lightning speech, to his true destiny. It was Arnaud Bernard. Clearly defined on the features of his face there appeared an honest desire to put aside an ancient grudge. Lifting one hand to impose silence on all, he took a step forward. Through what aberration did the count deceive himself by this gesture? Did he think that the Capitoul whose wife he had taken was advancing towards him to strike him? Or did he wish to put an end to it by making an irreparably menacing gesture. He retreated a little and half drew his sword. For a few seconds he remained face to face with Arnaud Bernard. Between them stood the strength of sleeping hatred, the mystery of a woman's memory where two men had shared their love. Inside their open jackets the blueish glow of weapons sparkled. Thibaut and I had rushed behind our master. I heard Laurent Guillaume whisper:
"The one who strikes first will have the advantage," and I noticed the hideous character of his face.

"It's your salutation that I want", shouted the count, with the tone of a man who's not sure what he's saying. "You'll thank me later for having saved your houses, your wives and daughters". In the pregnant silence that followed this speech, we heard Arnaud d'Escalquens exclaim:

"Especially our women!"

For sure he didn't want to make fun of the count's morals and was not thinking of Arnaud Bernard's wife. But everyone thought about it at once, every one pictured the blonde Alix Bernard, heroine of an unspoken drama, apparently still alive and mad, in a convent's cell in Toulouse. Under the mouldy Christ on the far wall, I saw Alix Bernard looking through my soul, with her golden hair and dead opal eyes. The lover and husband forever separated by the ghost. There was something like an occult presence that immobilized his arms, froze his anger. Then the count signaled us to follow him and we crossed the immobile assembly as if an enchantment had suddenly turned them all to stone.

* Pierre Vidal was amongst the most famous troubadours in the South of France. His happy adventures in the Orient were legendary.

III

Arriving by day I climbed the highest hill to contemplate the spread of the crusaders' enormous army. It was tumultuous, shapeless, and uncountable. It rolled on out of sight, glimmering light, ringing shouts, bristling with lances, crosses and banners. The whole left bank of the Rhône was occupied by German soldiers, commanded by the count of Bar. They used conical black tents that made one think of the dwellings of some monstrous termite. Many of them were drinking or washing themselves in the river alongside their horses. Most of them were on all fours dunking their red heads, whose size seemed oddly disproportionate to their armoured bodies. I saw their long wet beards and heard their ridiculous shrieks of laughter. They were having fun throwing sand and wrestling each other to the ground, resembling some strange iron clad quadrupeds.

The Bretons, Bourguignons, Swiss and Italians were spread out on the right hand banks. They formed neighbourhoods, like those of a city. The setting sun made the backs of their helmets glow like terrestrial stars. Circles of light sprouted from improvised forges and I could hear the noise of hammers ringing against steel. The paths in between the tents were crowded with dice players and quarrels were breaking out in differing tongues. Riders passed, carrying messages. A line of monks, in beige cassocks, snaked around an olive grove.

The King's banners marked out a quadrangle of fields for the religious. It encompassed a chapel where the bishops were giving mass. Unfortunately the crusaders' vanguard had pillaged it on arrival, ignoring the honor awaiting it. They had broken down the doors and even smashed the ornaments on the facade.

The church's bell was fractured; it gave off a sinister tone and in the sound of its angelus an atmosphere of malediction prevailed.

Beyond the Knights of Jerusalem and the Templars' camps, there stretched a sea of strange carts, disheveled tents and chariots hung with colored fabrics. Where the armies' parasites lived, the good time girls with their hustlers, the Vandals, the Gypsies and the beggars. They woke with the setting sun and multiplied before my eyes as if they had come out of some mysterious ants' nest. I heard foreign songs, barbarous music, savage arguments and sometimes the screams of a peasant woman being raped. In a few minutes, a bazaar had unfolded in an alley. Soldiers were pushing around a tent that was larger than the rest. Behind the rag drapes were smiling semi-nude girls. Buffoons were turning around in the middle of a circle. This moving, screaming, colorful crowd was churning around a tall phallus acting as its symbolic axis.

It was big Coesre's emblem. He was the king of the Vandals. With the king of France's permission he towed it behind his chariot. From where I sat, illuminated by the setting sun, the phallus was disproportionate, gigantic. It resembled a monstrous God belonging to a people deprived of reason. Just a little further, the metal cross that marked the envoy's camp was as tall, seemingly covered by the same gold and glowing just as bright. I couldn't take my eyes off the symbol of these two blind forces, desire and faith that were spilling over my country, to enslave it and plunder its wealth.

The three hundred cavalrymen the count of Toulouse had brought with him, under the banner of a black key on a golden cross, looked like a little diamond in a heap of rubbish. I was striding towards their camps and the men of my race when I got a violent shock in the chest and rolled over in the dust.

I'd been knocked down by a passing rider's horse, which followed by a few men-at-arms. The rider turned around, but without stopping.

I saw him, wearing no helmet; his head of short greying hair was astoundingly round, like a marble and curiously lacking eyes.

A voice said: "He's one of the count of Toulouse's men."

Then I saw under the rider's eyebrows a greenish line, which had the phosphorescence of a cats eyes in the darkness and I heard contemptuous laughter. The group disappeared at the turn in the road.

Full of rage, I jumped to my feet. I realized I was unarmed. I can't say what insults I was spitting out when a soldier, who was passing on foot and must have been a witness to the scene, approached me.

"You've obviously no idea who that rider was who knocked you over," he said.
"No, but if I did know..."
The soldier told me to be quiet and whispered:
"That's Simon de Montfort."

❁

I had always believed that the affinity for theft and the desire for riches were at the roots of war. I realized that they were futile. The possession of women is the propelling force that pushes men to fight. The only thing the soldiers were talking about was the beautiful women they were going to take from the conquered cities. The further we descended the Rhône and the closer we got to Occitania, something akin to a sexual hallucination raged like a ghost in the back of everyone's gaze.

The count of Toulouse was speaking to no one and could only support my presence. He seemed to hold it against his cavalry for obeying his orders and following the crusade against their brothers. Actually, many of them left us along the way.

85

It was close to Montpellier when we heard that Trencavel, viscount of Carcassonne and Béziers, was resolute in shutting the gates of his cities and defending them against the crusaders.

The count of Toulouse was not overly fond of his nephew, whose excessive courage outshone him.

When he heard of his decision, he put his head in his hands and cried. I never knew if it was because of the misfortune he saw coming or if he regretted not doing the same.

An army lead by the bishop of Bordeaux, made up of barons from the Perigord and the Limousin, joined the crusaders that had formed in Lyon. There came others from Tarn and the Black Mountains. This massive armoured ocean of crosses and horses spread out around Béziers' walls.

The city was bristling with fortresses and dominated a steep hill. We knew that before shutting himself in Carcassonne, Trencavel had brought in numerous disciplined troops. Béziers' bourgeoisie was known for the good organization of its militias. Noblemen from many of the surrounding castles had taken refuge there.

"The siege will take at least a year," I told Thibaut the night of our arrival, as we were sitting in front of our tent. "The inhabitants of Béziers will show the Northerners the virtues of Occitan blood." Thibaut just nodded his head in his habitual way. I heard someone burst out laughing next to me and turned to see Laurent Guillaume. We were forced to share our tent with him and despite our efforts to keep our distance, he was nearly always by our side.

"I believe that by sunset tomorrow the town will be in the crusaders' hands," he spouted. It was my turn to laugh at such a ridiculous affirmation. But he added with a calm certainty that since Arnaud, the pope's legate and the pious Simon de Montfort commanded the army, the walls would fall and the fighters scatter.

I asked him to take his sword and leave the camp with me. God would show us which one was right. He refused with an amiable smile, reciting the severe orders forbidding the crusaders from fighting amongst themselves.

"For you carry the cross," he added. "Thank God, who will protect you from death."

A large red cross was in fact sewn on the jerkin that I was wearing on top of my chain mail. Thibaut shook me awake the following morning.

"Something's going on," he told me. I heard a rumour that came rumbling from all sides at once. Laurent Guillaume was up and armed. He didn't even glance at us, but ran off, who knows where. In turn we put on our armour and went out.

The sun had barely risen. It was July and the heat was oppressive. Some riders passed next to us, accompanied by others on foot that were puffing and panting as they followed. Some were still fastening their armor. One had the feeling that they were in a rush. Everyone was heading in the same direction, towards the Narbonnais gate, the widest and most prone to attack. It was coming from over there, the confusion of furious shouts, neighing horses and the noise of clashing weapons that distant battles make.

"If we had decided to make an assault on the city, all the crusaders would have been warned," Thibaut told me with good sense. We were heading towards the count of Toulouse's tent to take his orders. It was on the other side of a small wheat field.

As we were crossing it, I saw a sergeant-at-arms who had one of those reddish faces common to Northerners. He couldn't run because of his large belly, that he carried in front of him with arrogance. He approached, full of dignity, spreading the wheat with his lance. I asked him what was going on. He was happy to have this occasion to catch his breath.

87

"One of Beziers' gates has just been forced open," he said with pride, as if it was him that the crusaders owed their thanks to for the exploit. "And do you know who forced it? It was the Vandals, lead by their king. To conquer Southerners you don't need soldiers. Vandals suffice! I think we must hurry if we're going to arrive in time for some loot." And off he waddled with his little steps.

Toulouse's cavalrymen were milling about the count's tent. Suddenly he appeared, half dressed. A lurid and sweaty man was holding out his hands and begging something of him. The count took his cavalry as witnesses.

"Well it's high time! Here's one of Béziers' bourgeoisie who's pleading me, in the name of his people to go and find Citeaux Abby and Simon de Montfort and save his city. Have you ever seen someone beseeching the wolves the moment they are about to jump on their prey?" More and more men-at-arms were pushing past us. The man from Béziers had fallen on his knees. He lifted his arms and his face was bathed in tears. The count was impatiently stamping his feet.

"Well! You should have done as I did! It's because I saw what was going to happen that I am here." The supplicant stammered something about his twenty-year-old daughter, sick and in her bed.

"So? Why didn't you escape? The bishop Reginald de Montpeyroux went around yesterday pleading with the citizens to leave Beziers. The Jews all left. Why did you not do the same? Men are so attached to their riches that apparently they prefer to die than abandon them." Thibaut meanwhile had gone to get the count's horse and had brought it next to him. Dumbfounded the count raised his voice to the point of shouting:

"But they all defy me. They all spite me. De Montfort will either accuse me of betrayal or he'll summon me to go and fight at his side. But where is he? Citeaux Abby is on the other side of the camp."

The count saddled up. The riders of Toulouse called for their horses to escort him. At that moment a deafening noise drowned out all others.

An immense column of pilgrims, belonging no doubt to the same religious brotherhood, was advancing towards Béziers singing canticles. The rhythm was slow and vast. It expressed the power of a formidable God and the obscure fatality of death, like the wave from a rip tide that suddenly surges, rising high and rolling in a long way across the barren strand. So did the crowd that followed them, uncountable, blind and singing, burst upon us, scattering us before them. I saw the count of Toulouse struggling to take control of his cohorts. I thought at first to join him by beating a path through the mob with my scabbard, but curiosity seized me and I let myself be taken in this torrent that carried me towards the gates of Béziers.

⚜

Even if they were still fighting at the Narbonnais gate, even if the bridge had been taken, it was by the Catalan gate that I entered the city with the pilgrims. During the walk, several of them tried to talk to me in a wild and incomprehensible language. I contented myself by showing them the big cross on my chest and the naked blade of my sword. They answered with strange cries, one showing me a huge pocket under his jacket, the other, a bag on his back. I saw by the expressions on their faces that they rejoiced at the thought of pillaging and were hoping to return laden with booty. They must have come from far away countries for nearly all of them were horribly red-haired. Next to me a thin man of extraordinary size was walking with his eyes uplifted repeating an unfamiliar woman's name, "Gunnur!" with such impassioned intonation that I thought he must have surely been referring to his betrothed. He had a fat face full of goodness and was carrying a short, wide and unusually shaped cutlass. Another, a sort of hairy dwarf, naked to the waist and with an axe propped across his shoulder resembled nothing more than one of those trolls from the Northerners' poems.

89

They formed small, quite disciplined groups of twenty or so to a team, obeying a man whose hair was redder than the others and whose lance, to rally them, bore a blue pennon.

There was no sign of fighting at the Catalan gate. It was already guarded by some of the count of Nevers' soldiers. They shouted to us as we passed that they had opened the gate by surprise and without resistance. They warned us to ready our weapons as there was fighting in all quarters of the city.

The roads we went up were dead and silent. All the doors were barred. My companions were walking slowly and with lowered voices, intimidated. We spilled out onto a little square which had a fountain in the middle, shaded by a plane tree. The noise of the water, the shade of the houses, the freshness of the air evoked memories of peaceful happiness. The place was so calm that a few pilgrims sat down on the edge of the fountains. Others were tempted to turn back.

Then a door opened and a woman came out of one of the houses. I could see that she looked well off. She took two or three steps and then saw us. She screamed: "Jesus Marie" and started running. No one moved. Only the skinny man with a good face shouted: "Gunnur!" and threw himself after her. He caught her up in three strides and struck her on the head with his cutlass. She crumbled and he hurled himself on her body, cutting her dress, searching her and almost cutting her fingers off to get her rings... Then he carefully put what he had taken into one of his pockets, shouting something that must have signified that it was his, as he gesticulated with arrogance.

For a few seconds, the pilgrims formed a circle around the woman whose blood ran onto the paving stones from the gaping wound in her head. They said nothing at first, standing stock still as if frozen by the sight. My first move was to throw myself on the assassin, but I stopped in my tracks. All those around me had just let out a wild scream as if driven into a homicidal fury by the hot, rich smell and color of that slow pooling crimson stain.

I saw the dwarf attacking a door with his axe. Others were giving each other a leg up to scale a little wall. Soon shrieks rang out in all the houses. Silent they might have been, but they were all full of their appalled residents.

A child that had been thrown out of a widow landed in the fountain amongst a spray of droplets. A man who was trying to rip out a dagger from his chest stumbled into me. A little further on, three oafs were arguing over a young girl who had the face of a Madonna, under her bedraggled black hair. One of them had put his knife under her collar to cut open her dress. He must have done it too brutally for as the dress tore it showed her body opened from top to bottom by the blade.

The crusaders were getting more and more numerous, arriving from all sides. The victims' cries rang out in a soul-destroying timbre. Furniture was being dragged into the streets, along with materials and casks. A young hero sat on a rooftop and shot at the crusaders with a bow, as little as a toy, killing several men around me. Methodically he took another arrow from the quiver he had placed beside him, and fired as if he were on the range, never missing his target. As I stared at his pale face framed by a mane of black hair, he nearly nailed me to a door. Out of all of those he aimed at, I was the only one he missed. The road soon emptied. None knew how to reach the rooftop where he sat. When his quiver was empty, he glanced around, got up calmly and disappeared, no doubt through some skylight. I wanted to shout out my admiration to that fine archer, but prudence held me back.

I stumbled haphazardly through the streets where mayhem reigned. Several times I was knocked over by horsemen. Sometimes some mad ones threw themselves at me and I had to parry their attack with my sword until they had distinguished the cross I wore on my chest. In the end I decided to cover myself in blood so that I looked like those who were already engaged in the massacre and therefore avoid being killed by them. I saw an open door and entered into a corridor then into a room with an appalling odour.

91

By a skylight's glow I saw a group of drunken soldiers lying next to some terrified, half naked women, whose eyes shone in the shadows. The soldiers took me for one of them and shouted that they had everything in abundance.

One of them pushed a bottle my way with his foot. As I took a step towards the women they cowered with fear and I saw a body covered in blood, lying motionless beside them. I distinguished with confusion the shadow of hair, the form of a graceful bust with a great red-black hole where her heart should have been. I lowered myself to my knees, soaking my hands in the blood that was flowing from the dead woman's ravaged breast; I ran my crimsoned fingers across my forehead and cheeks. I heard a peal of savage laughter.

"He prefers blood to wine." More laughter followed. The thought of drinking the blood didn't fill me with the disgust I might have felt a few hours earlier. I was caught up in a kind of drunkenness. I had breathed a wind that carried corruption. The taste of death passed through me. All I wanted now was to destroy and kill. I was like a zombie and driven senseless, feeding on the screams of hatred and despair, drawing a new and monstrous pleasure out of the subsoil of my flesh. I had the feeling some sort of hydra, a fantastic beast with teeth and tentacles, had been born in the depths of my heart, and was growing there. I was possessed by the ambient evil. I couldn't detach myself from it and suffered for being a part of this terrible beast.

They had carried all the wounded to a big square. It was said that a part of the city had defended itself. I learned that more than six thousand people had taken refuge in the Saint-Nazaire church. The crusaders had managed to throw some torches through the roof. The women's dresses caught fire. In turn they ran around, spreading the fire that was consuming them. The pews and wood at the heart of the church started burning, soon the whole church was afire. God had then come with a miracle! The cathedral walls had cracked for no apparent reason, and all the sinners that had sought refuge therein were instantly buried.

I was shattered. I felt my senses leaving me. At the bend in the road that must have been the main street and which was particularly badly hit, I heard shouts. The soldiers that surrounded me fell to their knees.

Those who were in the middle of pillaging the shops appeared red faced on the doorsteps. With their helmets hanging around their necks by the straps, they prostrated themselves.

Preceded by a sergeant-at-arms bearing an iron cross and followed at some distance by a group of Templar knights, a man, or maybe a ghost had just surged into this perspective of destruction. He wore the white robes of a Cistercian monk and was riding a white horse with a flowing mane. I first thought of Jesus Christ, then the angel Lucifer. I soon recognized this beautiful symmetrical face with its big nose and dark eyebrows that made one think of a perpetually angry Jupiter.

It was Arnaud, the pope's legate, Abbott of Citeaux, who commanded the crusaders armies with Simon de Montfort. He lifted his right hand with a regular, automatic gesture, like someone throwing manna. He blessed the murderers, the drunkards and the profane. He blessed the weapons that had slit throats. On all of them he heaped the invisible manna of spiritual rewards, the promise of eternal paradise.

In the middle of the Templars who rode behind the legate, I recognized his councilor and confidant, the Spanish monk Dominique, to whom miracles were attributed and who passed for a saint in the wider Christian world. His enormous and completely bald forehead was making a matt stain amongst the shiny light of the helmets. Where I stood, in the spot where the road bends there was a heap of bodies piled one on top of another, over which a leather tarpaulin had been thrown. But it was too narrow and let some mutilated feet and dislocated heads stick out, hair protruding, like sinister vegetation. Dominique's horse rubbed against a dead man's foot and reared up.

I followed the monk's gaze and understood that he didn't see the dead on which he had nearly fallen. He had the faculty of only seeing the living, those that wore the Red Cross on their chest. He saw me with my cross and his jaw stiffened with benevolence. He didn't turn his head to avoid seeing the pile of dead. They were invisible to him. I noticed a large, fresh blood stain on his robe and it stuck to his knee, but for the same reason, he probably felt neither the humidity nor smelt the odor.

I don't know for sure what happened to me in the hours that followed. At some point I must have lain down and fallen asleep, with that evil hydra stuck in my flesh, so alive in me, identifying itself so much with my soul that I would not have been surprised to find claws in the place of my fingernails and teeth sticking out of my chest.

When I woke, the setting sun was very low in the sky, casting a worryingly sulphurous glow by which I orientated myself to get out of the city. Looking to the east however I saw the glare of another sun seemingly settling into a whirling mass of ardent embers. A third sun shone in the north and a fourth in the south that sent massive sparks towards the darkening sky. There were suns on all four cardinal points.

I started running straightforward, prey to an enormous fear. Was I witnessing the cosmological phenomenon, which since time immemorial, had been spoken of as the precursor to the end of the world? Four fiery globes lit the miserable human world as if, to light up even the most secret folds of their souls. They gave off such a lively, sanguine light that I was able to untangle the inner book of my thoughts. I read my cowardice, my bewildered self-love, and the growth of evil that I hypocritically called curiosity. I was complicit in the crime, I had been witness to the lamb's slaughter and by rights I was going to share in the chastisement of the doomed.

With chattering teeth I stopped at a square, in front of a small church whose door was smoking.

It seemed to me that this smoke was creating the rainbow foretold by John in the apocalypse. I thought I saw on his throne the one who manifests in stones of jasper and sard. The twenty-four old men dressed in white were slowly leaving the church. The four mysterious animals were beating their leathery wings and starring at me with their uncountable eyes. Then another idea came to me. Someone had killed me as I slept. I was dead. This self extinguishing church, these grumbling open houses, these sinisterly stretching roads, all this was just the dreams of an errant soul in the after-world.

Hell had taken its shape from the last image of my life. I had mixed with assassins, I was one among them now and the archangel's sword would push me someplace, with the reprobates, against the Spaniard Dominique's bloody robe, against the Englishman Simon de Montfort's eye-less head. I was so scared that I began crying. Some shouts answered mine. Some other dead men were running next to me, in the horror of the four apocalyptic suns. One of them expressed in the language of the living that a fire, an earthly fire lit by human hands had been set in all four corners of the city.

"It's the Vandals!" They shouted. "They're fighting with the Italians for the women." Another said: "They've taken three hundred young girls, they are forcing them to walk with ropes around their necks, spiking them like wild beasts."

Then I came back to my senses. I considered the roads' appearances. I was still within the city of Béziers and I directed myself as best as I could, wanting at any price, to escape the funereal circle in which I was turning. Suddenly I recognized where I was. I recognized the little square, the fountain and the plane tree. I saw a corpse sitting up in the same spot, one of the admirable archer's victims. In the fountain the child's body, floated in the water, with open eyes. It had swollen and the face had become black and enormous like a monster. Some big flies were giving it a halo. The square, with the twilight and silence of the dead had found once again the peaceful calm that had impressed me in the morning.

I was very close to the Catalan Gate. I was heading down the road that led there when I heard a joyful shout and a name: "Gunnur!" I saw the pilgrim, whom I had walked beside with his cutlass. He recognized me and gave me a friendly wave. His face was still full of goodness but its color had turned earthy. He was dragging a chest behind him, where he had no doubt put his spoils. He showed me triumphantly. Amongst odd objects, half entwined in a golden candelabra, there was a woman's long plait that he must have cut off with his cutlass, as the end was all bloody. He saw what I was looking at and proudly pulled out the plait.

Without knowing why, I thought of Esclarmonde's divine hair. He must have thought that I was envious of such a possession as he let out a big laugh. Then, with all the strength in my arm, I struck him on the head with my sword, the same stroke that he had given the fleeing woman that morning. Only I struck him face on and shouted as loud as I could "Gunnur!" He fell flat on his face and stopped moving. The square had become more obscure and more silent as I set off at a run towards the Catalan Gate. I reached it without trouble but when I was far enough from the ramparts I took a little path that would join the road to Carcassonne, the opposite direction to the crusaders' camps.

I was thirsty and hungry and worn out. After I'd walked a long time and night had fallen, I sat down by the side of the road. In the distance one could make out the glow of the burning city and the contours of its carbonized skeleton. I could hear a desperate wailing that must have come from the women that the Vandals were raping. A shadow stretched out before me and I realized that I was crouching at the foot of a cross. I stood up and grabbed it, wrestling it with all my strength but its roots had been buried deep in the earth and resisted my efforts. In the end it gave way and I managed to rip it out and throw it to the ground. Then I tore off my doublet with its red cross and ripped it to pieces. Only then did I feel liberated from the monstrous beast that I had carried in my heart. Noticing that my sword's hilt was also shaped like a cross I picked up a stone and hit it until it was bent out of shape.

IV

I found it impossible to buy a horse in Narbonne. There were so many people fleeing the city that I couldn't have found one, even if I was willing to pay a fortune. A Jew sold me a donkey and with this I set off for Carcassonne.

The following morning, I was stopped by a group of the viscount's soldiers at the foot of Mount Alaric. They were only letting through those willing to fight. They saw, by the look that I gave them, that I was ready and they let me in.

It was very hot and I had dismounted to ease my donkey's burden. As I reached the ramparts, I noticed there were lookouts on the towers and the gateways were closed. Carcassonne, secure within in its Visigothic walls, was enclosed like a warrior in its stone armour. As I was getting ready to cross the drawbridge I passed some cavalry who were leaving the city. By the pennon they were flying I recognized that they belonged to the county of Foix. Behind them was a woman, covered from head to foot in a black robe. She turned around to wave at a small, shaven headed young man. He looked at her leaving, immobile, leaning on his sword and I recognized the unchanging features and dreamy eyes of Esclarmonde de Foix, viscountess of Gimoez.

With my disheveled beard, covered in dust and pulling my donkey by its bridle, I looked like such a miserable wretch that my first thought was to hide. But Esclarmonde caught up with a rider, with a peasant's face, who must have been her husband, the count of Gimoez and she passed without glancing at me.

I stared at her as she rode off, envying her escort for breathing the same air, for smelling the same dust. I would have happily given my life to hold her horse and to deliver a message written by her hand. A voice rudely interrupted my thoughts.

"Where are you going? Where the devil have you come from? I'm wondering who in hell let this beggar in!" I was in the presence of a short, stocky individual who, no doubt because of the heat, had unlaced his breastplate. He must have been a man of some importance as with a nod, two soldiers readied themselves at once to seize me. Without a doubt my attitude lacked respect as he shouted at me again:

"I am the lord of Espinouze, can you hear me?" I hurriedly answered that I was Dalmas Rochemaure, squire to the count of Toulouse and that I had come to fight alongside my countrymen. He tossed his head with a doubtful air and murmured a phrase that included the words 'spy' and 'prison' but at that moment the young man, whom Esclarmonde had waved to, approached, overhearing our conversation. Though he was wearing a soldier's thick linked haubergeon his movements were sprightly. This newcomer had a jolly attitude, full of spirit and from the respect that surrounded him, I recognized Roger Trencavel, viscount of Béziers and Carcassonne.

"Why not? He may well be one of my uncle's brave servants," he said turning towards an old but unusually dressed horseman with a long grey moustache and a look full of malice. I found out later that this was the famous Pierre de Cabaret, who had kept the habit, from his time in the Orient, of wearing a red turban, a stripy silk surcot and bearing a Moorish scimitar. Roger Trencavel signaled me to follow him beyond the second rampart, up to the foot of the Narbonnais tower. There he asked me to tell him everything I knew about the crusaders' armies and the destruction of Béziers.

I recounted all the scenes that I had witnessed. Whilst I was talking, he was tapping a flagstone with the tip of his sword. Taps that grew progressively harder.

When I had finished, he remained silent for a long while, sometimes glancing at me with the severest look, as if I'd personally unchained such great horrors. Then he turned to Pierre Cabaret and said:

"They will be here within a week." The old turbaned warrior leaned forward and whispered something, pointing at me. "Do you think so?" Said Trencavel. I felt goodwill shining out of him.

"He'll come with me", said Pierre de Cabaret. "I'll need him for the defense of the Samson tower."

⁂

Roger Trencavel had given each of his barons a tower to defend and Pierre de Cabaret was commanding the Samson tower. He had brought the men-at-arms from his chateau but there were barely thirty of them. He had also brought, intending to train them in the art of war, the craftsmen from the Treasury. These workers were part of an arrogant group that scorned the use of weapons, which had now become obligatory. I was given leadership over ten of them.

It was on the ninth day after my arrival that we saw, from the tops of the ramparts, the advance guard of the crusaders. For a whole day the enormous army, like a cloud of iron insects, swarmed around the city, totally surrounding her. The waters of the Aude which cut through their massed ranks, looked like a blue sword thrown across an ants nest.

The crusaders had left a big space free in between their front line and our ramparts. We never learned for sure how lord Espinouze, commander of the Narbonnais tower died. He had a bad habit of taking off his breastplate, due to his large stature, as it eased his breathing. He was apparently watching the sunset behind a battlement when an arrow, shot with incredible agility, pierced right through his stomach.

Roger Trencavel immediately gave the orders to keep cover.

The moneymakers used it as an excuse to show their ridiculous faint-heartedness by moving about on all fours.

Those that were under my orders took the opportunity to make fun of me behind my back, insulting my master the count of Toulouse, even insulting the people of Toulouse who, according to them, were fighting for the crusaders out of cowardice. I wanted to show these metal forgers that the soul of a Toulousan can be devoid of fear.

I knew my companions were great lovers of music and singing, so the night that followed the death of lord Espinouze, I borrowed a viola from one of them. As they were all assembled in the main hall of the Samson tower I told them that I needed celestial space and starlight above my head. I went out and sat on top of one of the battlements, out in the open with my legs dangling over the edge.

Accompanying myself on the viola I sung the ancient song of the violet that I had learned from a wandering minstrel, under an elm tree in the place Saint-Sernin. Among the gifts that remain strong, even without practice, I was blessed with a moving voice full of depth and strength. My song traveled far, across the divide, and reached the camps where the Northern men slept heavily, like cattle. Many who awoke in wonder, approached silently. As I finished I could see human silhouettes above the ditches in that ecstatic pose that is given to musical reverie.

Then, lifting the seven stringed viola, I stood up on the battlement. Expressing with the gesture of my arms, my joy at having created a few moments of truce, by the virtues of this song consecrated to beauty.

Just as the cowards from the Treasury shouted at me to take cover I lifted the viola up again. I was struck with a violence that threw me to the stone floor. An arrow, maybe shot by the same archer who had slain lord Espinouze, had struck me on the heart. Luckily I had put on my chain mail under my cloth justaucorps.

I spat over the ramparts to express my disgust at these savages who having profited from the song, tried to kill the singer.

We made sorties and in turn the crusaders attempted to storm the city. The two fortified suburbs, which stretched along the right bank of the Aude, were lost, taken, and burned one after the other.

Many brave men fell fighting. We saw in the distance the machines of war rising over the tents like fabulous beasts. The men who were placed in my command underwent a radical transformation. One was killed, several were wounded and all felt the proximity of death. Little by little their initial fears were transformed into a courage that almost equaled my own. At first I felt a secret bitterness but then I thought that it might have been due to my example although this was obviously admitted by no one.

Maybe that is how men are, from Marseilles to the sandy lands of pines, I thought - only showing their courage after an ostentatious spell of cowardice. This courage and our common love of music nearly cost us our lives. The workers of the Treasury had a habit, before the siege. A band of them would go in the evening to a small copse of laurel and figs on the outskirts of the city. There they sat and listened to the voice of an extraordinary nightingale who had taken to living in an ancient and singular oak. Now they were deprived of the song as the little wood was situated closer to the camps than the city.

As soon as night fell, they listened for the faint echo of that marvelous song. In the end a big man named Samatan whose spirit seemed as broad as his body declared that he'd rather die than not hear the nightingale sing. Without thinking that anyone would accept I audaciously proposed to sneak out of the city and go to the little wood under the cover of darkness. Those that stayed would hold the gate ajar and await our return.

To my great surprise, many of these music loving metal smiths accepted with joy and I couldn't go back on my word. The July nights are particularly serene. Fifteen of us left, bent double and scuttling from bush to bush. We reached the little wood without raising the alarm from either the camps' or the city's sentinels. We waited there for over an hour in silence, our spirits kept up by Samatan's frog imitations that he reckoned incited the nightingale to sing.

At last it sang and by the prestige of its inhuman melody we were transported into a celestial universe. When the marvelous bird stopped, its silence spread such a great melancholy upon us that war, the Cathar heresy or even death appeared completely devoid of importance.

As I saw the sadness on the shadowy faces of my companions I was moved to resume the song of the nightingale in my own voice and bring them back the dream they had tasted and lost. Giving it all I had, I burst into the first verse of the song of the violet. As soon as I had started singing, my companions threw themselves on me as the nearest camp had detected our presence and we were surrounded. Arrows whistled from all sides and men with sparkling breast plates descended upon us. The divine bird took flight at the sound of their savage war cries. My companions fell around me as I managed to parry the first lunges, making the shadows retreat in front of me. Only Samatan and I succeeded in breaking through the enemy lines. We started running towards Carcassonne with all our strength. I gave him an arm for support as he ran, as his enormous weight caused him great difficulty.

We arrived alone at the Samson tower and waited in vain for our companions. Pierre de Cabaret, woken by the noise, appeared scimitar in hand. He assured me that for having led this expedition I would be transferred the following day to the prison tower. But more serious events must have turned his attention away from my chastisement.

The following morning, a gigantic knight astride an enormous horse, was prancing in front of the ramparts of the Narbonnais tower. He was so totally covered in armour that we didn't even think of firing arrows at him. He was proffering insults and demanding to engage one of Carcassonne's knights in single combat.

The whole town had come out on the ramparts to see him. As I arrived I heard the viscount of Béziers shouting for his horse and his weapons. But Pierre de Cabaret as well as several other barons ran to him, gesticulating, and he bowed down from the fight.

I wasn't a knight but recognized my opportunity to escape going to prison. If I suddenly ran out and confronted this monstrous knight he would not be able to refuse engaging me. I was on my way to the Samson tower to pick out a horse when an adolescent, so small he would look like a dwarf next to the enemy whom he was preparing to fight accosted me. He had been hastily given an outsized breastplate and helmet, which was obviously not his. His lance on the other hand was ridiculously small. He passed next to me amongst the people running and shouting with enthusiasm. I heard someone say that it was lord Espinouze's son. The drawbridge had just lowered and I ran to the ramparts to see what was about to unfold.

The crusaders in the distance fell silent, forming an unbroken line. The combat lasted only a few seconds and the assistants on both sides barely had time to realize what had happened.

The young Espinouze took off with all the speed his horse could muster. He struck his immobile enemy who sent his lance flying with the first stroke. The two horses started spinning round, trying to bite each other. For in battle, animals take the sides of their masters and if they could talk, they would shout out a myriad of wise council and events would make about turns based on their advice.

Amidst the swirling dust we could see that the two badly matched combatants had drawn their swords.

All of a sudden there came an enormous gasp of stupefaction, both from the crusaders and the inhabitants of Carcassonne. None had doubted the victory of the gigantic warrior over the child and we had let the latter go like a propitiatory sacrifice to the mysterious God of war, who so loves useless heroics. As if by a bolt of lightning the admirable Espinouze's sword pierced the crusader's throat.

It must have taken an extraordinary piece of luck for the point of the blade to find the only susceptible millimeter in the seemingly impenetrable armour. The knight crumbled and his horse took flight in shame.

The whole city of Carcassonne formed two human rows behind the drawbridge, under the Narbonnais gate's arcade, to deliriously welcome the returning hero. His mother, a white haired woman, large and strong, was standing next to the viscount of Béziers, who was getting ready to grab the victorious child's bridle.

On all sides they were shouting.
"It's David who slew Goliath!"

But he came in slowly, for one who had ridden out so fast! There was some bumbling uncertainty about him. He had even let go of his horse's reins. When he crossed the drawbridge the acclamations froze on their lips. The faithful horse stopped in front of the mother. What had been brought back was dead.

David had killed Goliath, but in so doing David had perished too.

V

That year there was an exceptional heat wave that ran all the wells dry. A few people took advantage of this by only drinking wine, which they had in abundance in their cellars and consequently were constantly drunk.

The assaults were continuous and our small group of beleaguered fighters were obliged to run from one tower to the next depending on the attacks and soon ended up being worn out. As if this were not enough a strange illness spread through the city, making those affected lethargic; then with their souls in distress, they died within three days.

As the cemetery was situated outside the ramparts, the viscount ordered that the graves should be dug in the courtyards and public squares, turning the city into a vast necropolis. People were saying that they would be happy if they could leave the city with only the shirts on their backs, a reckless wish that would soon be realized.

That morning, with the rising sun, a bishop accompanied by some auxiliaries carrying crosses approached the foot of the Narbonnais tower to parley. I counted a dozen metal crucifixes fastened protectively around the bishop's mitre. The cortege moved off after a little while and the rumour spread throughout the city that Arnaud, abbot of Citeaux and Simon de Montfort, commander of the crusade, were asking Roger Trencavel to come and talk with them about an honourable capitulation under the safety of their oath. It was specified that in order to avoid his escort quarreling with the crusaders, he had to come to the camp alone, with a single squire.

From all sides of the city the inhabitants ran towards the castle's entrance along with the knights and men at arms. When the viscount appeared on horseback, the crowd fell to their knees, begging him not to believe the word of those who massacred the sixty thousand inhabitants of Béziers, shouting that the bishop and his oaths were not a sufficient guarantee. Roger Trencavel, pale and calm, tried to reassure his people and his soldiers by the tranquility of his demeanor.

"I'll be back in an hour at the most," he said. Bare headed and unarmed, wearing only a simple doublet, he made his way slowly through the crowd. When he had passed the drawbridge and started galloping towards the camp, he turned around and with his black gloved hand, made a friendly gesture towards his city. The same gesture of farewell that one makes to a mistress one will never see again.

Pierre de Cabaret, whom I was standing next to, was twisting his white moustache so much that I thought he might tear it off. As we feared no attack, the crowd had invaded the ramparts. Towards noon, a mendicant who was said to be a visionary, started a horrible howling, for no apparent reason but as we tried to calm her she took off running. With her hair undone, she looked like a sleep- walker. Then she crumpled at the foot of the Tresau tower, from where her wailing rose for some time, chilling our hearts with fear.

We were still waiting in vain as the sun began to set. Then a murmuring grew in the far distance. It spread and rose through the crusader's army, reaching the furthest outposts of the camp, where the hangers on, the traders, minstrels and entertainers had found shelter. This murmur became ebullient, like an enormous wave of joy, as if they had all taken part in a massive practical joke. We saw men run out into the open and make obscene gestures towards Carcassonne. It was time for lighting the fires for the evening meal and through the distant flickering flames; we could make out silhouettes, roaring with laughter and dancing grotesquely, even the machines of war looked like drunken happy giants.

106

It was as if the heroic city's heart had broken. All the creatures within its stone enclosure let out a singular wail that climbed towards the newborn stars. Nobody doubted the treachery, or the city's loss. There were very few that fell to their knees. People wept on their feet and you could see the despair in the depths of their eyes, like a non-existent landscape with an endless perspective.

"Come," said Pierre de Cabaret as he swept past me. I saw that he had just called Hebrew Nathan who had been chosen to organize the catapults due to his mechanical knowledge. I heard him say in a muffled voice:

"We can still save everyone." We congregated in the chateau's main hall, where the Bellissen brothers, the lords of Avignonnet, Bram and Beauxhoste, Sarraut the armourer, Camus the butcher and the city's Principal were already gathered. Everyone agreed that the crusaders, profiting from our distress, would attack at dawn. It was only Camus the butcher who proposed surrender. The others wanted to make an all out attack and die fighting. Then Pierre de Cabaret explained that long ago, Roger Trencavel's father and his own father had built a tunnel leading from Carcassonne to Cabardez, fiefdom of the Cabarets.

As soon as he had heard about the crusade, Roger Trencavel had repaired this tunnel, which was several leagues in length and which had in several places caved in. All the inhabitants could escape this way, but it would certainly take the whole night.

Each of us got the task to warn a district and lead them to the tunnel, whose entrance was in the chateau's basement. The clamour of desperation quietened little by little and made way for sighs and whisperings of hope. Many who had preparing for their deaths were overcome by joie de vivre. Within the hour a crowd clutching bags, stacks of provisions, old clothes and even furniture ringed the chateau. A potter presented himself with a donkey laden with wares. He begged and pleaded saying that he cherished his ass as much as himself. It was his best and oldest friend.

However, I was almost sure I recognised the donkey as the very one I rode into Carcassonne, a few days previously.

Everyone had to leave anything that would slow down the exodus. Pierre de Cabaret had to unsheathe his scimitar and swear to put to death anyone who presented themselves with any sort of bag on their back. There were some who returned to their houses, preferring to face the fate of the inhabitants of Béziers rather than give up their possessions.

Late in the evening, a never-ending human snake had already dug itself deep into the earth's mantle. Pierre de Cabaret charged me with going round the houses making sure there wasn't any one crippled or deaf who had been left behind.

I met an old and bald man in the city who was carrying an enormous bundle of arrows under his arm. He was off to barricade his house and he explained that as soon as the crusaders arrived, he meant to put as many to death as was in his powers. A family was peacefully asleep in a basement flat. A candle was burning next to the timeworn statue of some nameless saint. They wouldn't get up, regardless of my pleading. The father shouted out that he was at peace. Nothing bad could happen to them. The Saint would protect them.

The night was drawing to an end. The city was abandoned as I made my way back to the chateau to find Pierre de Cabaret on the doorstep with a few loyal cohorts who were preparing to go down the tunnel. One of the Bellissen brothers arrived at a run and said that lord de Canacaude's widow was refusing to leave. He added, somewhat scandalised, that she was looking forward to the crusaders coming and was actively making preparations for their arrival. The name de Canacaude was a respected name. Lord de Canacaude had been a friend of Pierre de Cabaret and the old viscount Trencavel. He had fought alongside them in the Orient, but had died last year; I was told, of a sudden shock, apparently caused by his wife.

By the way people raised their arms, I understood that she was known for her easy conduct and eccentricity.

"You, you're a good looking lad," Pierre de Cabaret told me, "go and try to persuade her to follow us. Only be quick, for the day is upon us and the crusaders could be here within an hour."

The lady de Canacaude lived in one of the most beautiful houses in the city, opposite the Saint-Nazaire church. I ran along the empty streets, but as I didn't know the area that well I was forced to retrace my steps, which wasted some time. Under the light that precedes dawn the church of Saint-Nazaire looked like an immense pallid ghost whose stones oozed despair. The door was open and the interior was cocooned in mysterious shadows whose heart lay at the feet of the apse's twelve apostles. The square, transformed into a cemetery, was scattered with crosses. On the other side, facing this funereal landscape, I spotted lady de Canacaude behind a narrow stone balcony on the ground floor of her house. A cross that was taller than the rest rose close beside her. Her hand nonchalantly stretched out, gave the impression that she wanted to pick it like a flower from this strange garden. She was covered in rouge and blusher. Black locks of hair had been artistically arranged next to her temples and she tried to smile in an engaging manner. Behind her, the dawn light illuminated the four posts of an open bed surrounded by carafes of wine and gold brocades.

In a halting voice I repeated Pierre de Cabaret's order pleading with her to leave the city. She answered, showing me all her teeth, having learned from her venerable husband that a lady de Canacaude had nothing to fear. I believed for an instant in her heroism but I felt it my duty to tell her how the noblest women were treated in Béziers. I spoke without blushing. She contented herself by raising her eyes and saying that God would look after her. Then I read in her soul that she was driven, like most people, to side with the winners. I wondered if I should chase this shallow caricature to the tunnel with the point of my sword.

Then all of a sudden a lassitude overcame me as if this female betrayal had caused an internal wound to overflow. I felt nothing for the human passion that surrounded me. The destruction of cities, the religious furore, the massacre of innocent creatures became strange to me. I no longer understood the cause that pushed men against each other. I felt sad and lonely, adrift in an incomprehensible desert.

A dog let out a dying howl not far away and I caught sight of some birds flying at a prodigious height. I became captivated by this flight for a few minutes, as if the whole universe turned around it. A greenish light was spreading in which the church and the house's stones, indeed the earth itself, seemed to be already decomposing. I lay down, with my head against a grave. Everything appeared to be in vain and the freshness of the soil on my cheek gave me a foretaste of my own desirable death. Then, in the clarity of the dream within which I was swimming, like a fantastic beast, the donkey laden with pottery, my donkey slowly crossed the tomb-laden square and sniffed the church steps before disappearing through the open doors.

I leapt up without being able to explain why but this donkey's journey had woken some hidden strength in me. From an infinite distance I made out the sound of a trumpet resonating in the silence of the rising sun. I started running as fast as I could towards the chateau. Outside it was completely deserted. I went in, listening for some sign of life from the tunnels below. I rushed down the winding staircase to find myself in front of Hebrew Nathan. He was in charge of a small band of men who were demolishing the tunnel supports in order to seal the passageway.

"Another minute would have been too late," he told me nodding his head as if it was a matter of little importance. I threw myself down the tunnel. The beams that were supporting the sides had been ripped out for at least a hundred meters. There were lanterns placed one after the other. The crowd that had just passed had left a vile odor. In a few places water was seeping through the roof.

I would never have believed that sunlight was so desirable and necessary for life.

After walking for a long while I found myself in front of a staircase of interminable length. Quite a few of the steps were missing forcing me to crawl on all fours. It felt like it was taking hours and I thought that this staircase was so long that it must have been cut into the flanks of a mountain. At length I detected a faint, pink glow from up ahead. The staircase made a sudden turn and at last the end of the tunnel came in sight. I nearly let myself fall to the floor in relief but instead I straightened my back and shook the earth from my hair. Three radiantly beautiful women were waiting to welcome me.

* The cities and chateau's of the Midi all had extensive tunnel systems. It was Arabic engineers who had taught the construction techniques.

VI

I'd heard much talk about the three extraordinary women who received me. Their beauty was renowned and it had spread throughout the crusaders' army. One evening on the banks of the Rhône I had witnessed several knights from Bourgogne and some hairy Bretons fantasizing about them. They had even played dice for their future possession, as if Goddess' were not always sheltered from the desires of rams and wild boars.

There were three of them and the three tall towers of the Cabardez carried their names. Brunissende was Pierre de Cabaret's wife. Nova was the daughter from his first marriage and Stéphania had married his oldest son, who had unfortunately died the first morning of their honeymoon. Brunissende had dark hair, like an evening on the slopes of the black mountains. Nova's was the golden color of sunlit heather. Smiling Stéphania's resembled a piece of amber, sculpted by a genius. All three dressed in similar immaculate linen dresses. The rumors ran that in the fervor of their Cathar mysticism they had vowed themselves to chastity.

The inhabitants of Carcassonne dispersed themselves throughout the vast lands of the Languedoc. Pierre de Cabaret only kept a few families in his chateau and the necessary fighters needed to defend this inaccessible spot, squeezed in by the torrents of the Orbiel. Naturally I was amongst them.

In the south, when one walks in this desolate region, one finds hidden behind the crag of a mountain, a friendly little village, with its fountains and inns. So too on my warrior's path I came across a place so beautiful it left me spellbound.

112

I shared my room with some knights from Carcassonne. It was situated next to the baths. One morning I walked passed the three marvelous creatures. They had that languor that women have when they get out of the bath and their wet hair almost hung to their feet. Brunissende's lips were pursed, Nova's eyelids' fluttered and Stéphania had trouble keeping a straight face. They strolled by casually, but the sign of predestined love had appeared for us. I loved all three of them from this day on, but with a mysterious association. In my thoughts I saw them with a single face that through some bizarre illusion recalled the features of Esclarmonde de Foix. Nevertheless I carried in my heart the devotion to a single unique beauty that was clothed in three human aspects.

I was teaching peasants to throw stones with a slingshot and to handle a crossbow. I went to a neighboring farm with a few men and escorted the cart loaded with grain and forage. If I turned around I almost always saw, in a window, in a tower or on a rampart, a figure in a linen dress following me with her gaze. I didn't know if it was Brunissende, Nova or Stéphania. I was suffused with that buoyancy given by the presentiment of love.

Everyone in Cabardez castle was practicing the Albigensian heresy. A beam had been nailed on the chapel door to prevent anyone entering. The chapel gave onto a small promontory from where one could survey the surrounding countryside. I went there every evening, happily watching the whirling night birds, listening to Orbiel's gurgling waters at the bottom of the cliffs.

An old white haired soldier who had accompanied Pierre de Cabaret in the Orient came when everything was quiet in the castle and knelt in front of the chapel door. Immobile like a statue, he prayed for a long time, and then left as he had come.

The three beauties from Cabardez toured the ramparts after the evening meal. They were once a little delayed and when they passed the church they saw both the old soldier kneeling and myself with my elbows on the balustrade.

They stopped but showed no visible emotion. I saw them confer for a few moments. Then with a neutral voice Brunissende called me over and asked me if I could help her remove the beam that was blocking the chapel door. It was poorly fixed and I managed to pry it free without trouble. They led the old man in, telling him to pray in peace, according to his faith. I even heard Brunissende add that wherever Albigensians were masters, everyone had the right to believe, true to their spirit, without fear of persecution.

They remained in front of the door, under their white cloaks, like angels on a nocturnal round. I felt very confused and divided so I said, with the sole aim of breaking the silence that I'd like to be more knowledgeable about this new religion, as there were certain things I just couldn't reasonably accept about it. Stéphania cheerfully asked me what these things were.

"I can't believe that life is as bad and diabolic as the pure Albigensians teach, for when I see certain faces so full of beauty, their contemplation gives me reason to live." I looked at them in a way that made it obvious that I was talking about them. They laughed innocently and Brunissende told me they knew just the person who would be able to explain the mysteries of their faith. They promised to ask this very wise man to speak to me the following day and all three wandered off still laughing, no doubt to retain their composure and hide their emotions

I knew that an Albigensian parfait, who was believed to be a great saint, lived in a perpetual state of deep meditation in a little room in one of the towers. It was said that he could see into the future by looking into a simple flat mirror just like those Arabic magicians. I didn't think that Brunissende took me seriously but the following day at the same time I found myself near the chapel, hoping to have the same meeting as the previous night. Then, I saw a small ageless man walking towards me, whose face was so pale that it seemed transparent. At first I was tempted to avert my eyes but he approached me, calling me brother and told me in a soft voice, that if I had a question to ask him he would happily answer it.

I babbled I'm not sure what words, in an attempt to cover the disappointment of meeting him instead of the beautiful creatures I was hoping for. When his eyes rested on mine they were distracted and it seemed that with the beating of his eyelids, he was trying to master the moist fog that precedes tears.

"It's not necessary for you to know more, for the moment," he said seemingly thinking about it deeply. "Man kills and in turn is killed. He forges for himself a chain of evil, which has no end, but he will have to untie all the knots, and with such pain! There's no point giving sight to one that is not yet ready to see. Follow your path, which is the longest and hardest and be content to make an effort every day to forgive others and forgive yourself." He looked at me with enormous pity and I left the chapel disappointed.

Winter had started blowing in the cypresses that clung to the slopes below Cabardez castle when Jordette Altaripa died. She was the daughter of one of Carcassonne's consuls and she had a tender love for the viscount Roger Trencavel. Having almost dragged her out by force, Pierre de Cabaret had put her in the most beautiful room in Cabardez castle. She never left it and every day she stayed by the window, looking out over the road to Carcassonne in the hope that a peasant or some traders might be bringing news.

During the autumn, we had heard all about the events that had taken place amongst the crusaders. The count Raymond had returned to Toulouse with his cavalry and I knew his feelings well enough to know that he would be full of remorse. After the pillage of Carcassonne and the repossession of its houses by strange stealing hands, the pope's legate and the Christian barons had proclaimed Simon de Montfort lord of all the lands conquered by the crusaders. The true master of these lands, Roger Trencavel, was shut in his own castle's prison. Did he shed bitter tears for his excessive trust?

Did he wish to die? Did he talk with Jordette Altaripa, his love, during his last hours, as she had believed? No one ever found out.

In the run up to Christmas, Jordette Altaripa moaned softly and ceaselessly, holding out her hands towards an absent companion. Lying with crossed arms on the crimson brocades of her bed, she looked like a dove crucified in blood. She didn't want any light to pass through her window, so that she might suffer the dense darkness that surrounded the one she loved. Sometimes she asked him a question as if he was there and she seemed to hear an unexpressed answer. She asked: "Do you still love me? Are you suffering not having me by your side?" Most of her questions were of a similar, simple nature but sometimes they were about something more precise, such as the place he was held, the possibility of overcoming the guards, how he was being treated. The non-resonating answers she perceived threw her into a deeper desolation.

There came a time when she refused to eat and even broke the cup and bowl that was offered to her, saying that the one she loved no longer received food or water and had been left to languish in his isolated cell.

One evening at sunset, the women who were looking after her in the darkness heard her utter a weak cry. She had died holding an invisible person against her. We learnt the following day that Simon de Montfort had, without any explanation, let it be known in Carcassonne that Roger Trencavel was dead. He was buried in the church of Saint-Nazaire with a certain pomp. Nobody doubted that he had starved to death in his own prison, the legitimate owner of the lands of Béziers and Carcassonne*.

* The Pope Innocent III mentions this murder in one of his letters and qualifies it as a "violent death".

116

VII

Cabardez castle was full of troubled souls. Grief had a strange effect on Pierre de Cabaret. He now dressed from head to toe in Arabic clothing and started swearing in Syrian. No one understood but he carried on regardless, inspecting the works on the defenses or the men practicing with their weapons.

Brunissende, Nova and Stéphania let no sadness show. "Death is a blessing", they said, "as it enables us to reach a state of purity that is happier than life. When those we love shed their material form, we should rejoice for them." They did have a revivifying effect, but I wasn't sure that the reasons for this were entirely spiritual. I was tempted to believe instead that this good humor was caused by something rather more human. Maybe it was because of me that there was the dawning flame of love in the three young women's eyes. Invisible smiles when we met, barely perceptible movements of the head were all certain proof. But what was going to happen? They were three and the greatest affection united them. Was I going to cause their separation? How was I to distinguish which one I loved most?

One morning I heard the enormous kettle drum and the trumpets ring out from the southern tower, where Pierre de Cabaret had installed them. They were strange joyful sounding instruments that he had brought back from the Orient.

It was agreed that they should resound when the first of the crusaders' armies came over the horizon. The music would symbolize, according to him, the joy he would have fighting the northern barbarians.

I was in the main courtyard and was rushing to my post in the western tower when, out of a basement, came the Albigensian parfait with whom I'd had that rather incomprehensible conversation. He signaled me with his hand and said softly:

"Dalmas Rochemaure, you must leave." Then he went off. Why did he tell me that? Why should I go the moment the castle needed all hands for its defense?

As I was asking these questions, Pierre de Cabaret came out of the same basement. He had just been conferring with the lords of Peixora and Bram, who had arrived from their castles and whose horses were even now steaming in the courtyard. He held a sealed scroll in his hand and upon seeing me shouted out one of his Arabic swear words to express his satisfaction.

Before the place was surrounded and the roads blocked, I had to return to Toulouse by way of the black mountains and the planes of the Lauraguais. No one was in a better position than me to speak to count Raymond, to give him the details of the events and to show him how much it was in his interest to come to the rescue of his besieged vassals. But on all sides the crusaders' helmets were shining. It would take a fast horse and a brave man.

That man was I. The drawbridge rose and with the clamor of trumpets in the air, I scrambled down the single path that clung to Cabardez's flanks. At the bottom of the path there was a crossroads with a circle of cypress trees and a rock shaped like a dog. It was here that I risked being taken or killed to adorn the Orbiel's blue waters as a burial shroud. I thought that, with consideration for the messenger, they could have decided on the message half an hour earlier.

I made it through the crossroads without being attacked. Either there was no one behind the cypresses or the stone dog, or they preferred to remain hidden and observe their enemy from afar. Then, I was all of a sudden illuminated with a certainty.

I was loved by Brunissende, by Nova and by Stéphania. Each of them confided in the wise Albigensian who in his wisdom, seeing the troubles and rivalry brought on by love, had told me in a peremptory tone: "Dalmas Rochemaure, you must leave!" Perhaps the wise Albigensian having taken part in the discussions between Pierre de Cabaret and the lords of Peixora and Bram, knew the order that was about to be given and had tried to warn me but I rejected this hypotheses as the least likely.

I looked back. Very far away, on the highest tower, to the trumpets fading song, I saw, well I thought I saw, three white figures. I didn't need to turn around to see them. I saw them most clearly with closed eyes and all three looked like Esclarmonde. Haunted by this unique image of ideal feminine beauty, I rode all day towards my new destination, far from the chateau of Cabardez, whose three marvelous feudal ladies* I feared were now forever lost to me.

⛨

*The crusaders besieged Cabardez castle a few months after the fall of Carcassonne, but it resisted all the onslaughts and Simon de Montfort was forced to abandon the siege. In the aftermath, due to his cunning, Pierre de Cabaret always managed to avoid the vengeance of the crusader's leader.

VIII

I saw the Antichrist, as he was called, in the lands of Toulouse, Albi and Foix. Pope Innocent III wasn't born of the tribe of Dan, as the prophecies had foreseen. He didn't heal the cripples or have demons as servants. His face was not revoltingly ugly, as I had naively believed. I was amazed instead to find that the man, who had consciously unleashed the calamity of war, had intelligent eyes and the sort of refined features that one sometimes sees on old Roman coins.

When I arrived in Toulouse, my horse was steaming so much that I found myself in a thick fog. At first the people on the Narbonnais gate didn't recognize me but as soon as they did, I was led to count Raymond. He was walking to and fro dictating his will to the lawyer Pierre Arnaud who sat at a marble table, his nose on the parchment due to his myopia.

"Whoever goes to Rome must first make his will," he said sadly, just as I was coming in. He considered the message I brought from Pierre de Cabaret as if it was completely devoid of importance. He even crumpled it as he looked upon me with satisfaction and a smile lit up his withdrawn face, my return obviously cheering him up.

"Every-one thought that you had died in Béziers." Suddenly a thought sprung from his soul, such an agreeable thought that he wanted to rejoice immediately for having it. He went to the door and shouted for some very dry Comminges wine.

"I know," he told me with a wink of an eye, "how much you detest sweet wine."

There was nothing to it but he had got that idea stuck in his head and there was little use trying to contradict him over something so puerile.

"You must come with me to Rome," he shouted, "Dalmas Rochemaure, my squire, will accompany me to stand before pope Innocent III. Nothing can change my mind." He repeated it joyfully, savoring the enormous irony of taking Pierre de Castelnau's murderer with him, to visit the pope. If he was going to Rome it was as much to complain about Simon de Montfort and his crusaders' crimes, as to rid himself of the accusation for Pierre de Castelnau's assassination. This accusation weighed heavily upon him. It was upheld by all the clergy in the Midi, and had spread throughout the Christian world. No proof had ever been found. I was, of all men on earth, the one who knew how false this accusation really was.

"I will have you blessed by the pope," he said putting a hand on my shoulder. He added after a while, in a less positive tone: "That is if I survive the poison, for apparently a lot of people are getting poisoned over there these days."

In Rome we made our way to the palace that Guillaume de Baux, prince of Orange owned and that he'd let my master use. Whilst waiting for an audience with the pope, the poison story played a big part. Under the pretext that I was a wine connoisseur, the count made me drink before him and then he looked out for the incipient signs of a rapid death. He always chose this moment to count out the enemies he had in Rome and in whose interest it was to see him disappear. I let out a big sigh of relief when the count, after waiting a month, was summoned to the Saint-Jean basilica.

Since his arrival he hadn't stopped writing a manuscript of complaints he was counting on bringing up in front of Innocent. He had resolved to learn it by heart and then to simulate an improvisation but his memory was rebellious. He feared being struck dumb at the last minute. In the end he decided to read his manuscript instead.

He was very worried about the costume he should wear, the way he should greet him, the etiquette. Bernard des Baux, the prince of Orange's brother, who was intimate with the pope, gave him some advice and promised to accompany him. He had to present himself without escort, dressed modestly, enter with bare feet and head straight into the Saint-Jean basilica. Dressed in the same manner, I would carry his coat and the manuscript of complaints, but I had to be careful to stay at the end of the church, in the part kept for the common folk.

Since Innocent's accession all official receptions were public but Bernard des Baux insisted there was no reason for alarm. As the count was terrified, not knowing the pope, that he might fall on his knees before a cardinal or even some ecclesiastical clerk, it was agreed that Bernard des Baux would hold him by the arm and lead him to Innocent.

On the morning of the ceremony, however, the count waited in vain for Bernard des Baux. This absence dismayed him extraordinarily. He thought it was treachery and told me that he was being summoned to be assassinated. This Bernard des Baux was a hypocrite who nurtured a great admiration for Simon de Montfort. He called for some wine. On calling me to taste it, I didn't have the heart to support his anxiety and I knocked the bottle over. The count considered this an omen and refused to drink it. He thought about presenting himself in the Saint-Jean basilica with sword and breastplate and he even ordered me to bring a crossbow on my shoulder. Then he wanted the horses saddled to leave this doomed city as soon as possible. He resigned himself at the last minute and I climbed aboard a run-down carriage that belonged to the des Baux palace.

An extraordinary crowd had invaded the place Saint-Jean and the precincts of the basilica. The count thought the coachman had mistaken the church and wanted to make him turn around. It was an ugly crowd, disrespectful and monstrous, the like of which I had never seen before.

The crowd made the law here in Rome, imposing its candidates for the papacy and massacring cardinals if they were dissatisfied with their vote. We passed through the mob, not without trouble, surrounded by swearing Italians, which we luckily did not understand.

As if by enchantment, the second my master ordered the coachman to turn around, the basilica's bronze doors swung wide before us. Armed guards jumped in front of the rearing crowd. The count of Toulouse advanced with uncertain steps on the cracked mosaics. I remained rooted to the spot, astonished by the sight of ten thousand candles, flickering in the cavernous, gilded chapels.

A door between two pillars, which gave onto the Latran palace, opened suddenly. I saw a single file of silent figures entering with automated movements and faces that looked as if they were set in stone. Each of them stopped in front of the main altar, bowing mechanically before taking their assigned places in a circle around it. They wore black jackets over violet mozettas and a quadrangular bar that reached down to their eyes covered their foreheads. Their tights and shoes were as red as if they had dipped them in a blood bath. They were the cardinals. I counted eleven cardinal-bishops, eighteen cardinal-priests and twenty-four cardinal-deacons. There were also officers from the apostolic chambers and other ecclesiastical bureaucrats in white, black, and violet robes bearing sparkling bands and shining crosses on their chests and in their ghostly waxen hands.

A majestic looking cardinal carrying the archbishop's pallium entered last. I thought it was the pope. He seemed astonishingly young. I heard voices in the crowd saying that he was the cardinal's deacon and I thought they were joking but in fact he was none other than the Ostie-cardinal who blesses the pope after his election and carries the title of deacon regardless of his age. The count of Toulouse had fallen to his knees before the altar. He was fervently pretending to pray. I only saw him from behind and could barley imagine the anguish he was feeling.

Yet providence was protecting him, for if he'd turned his head and seen the Ostie-cardinal he would doubtless have taken him for the pope and prostrated himself before him.

All of a sudden, something like the passing of an occult wind seemed to ripple through the basilica. A wave of silence immobilized the assembly. A monk bustled in from the door from whence the cardinals had entered and to my utter amazement headed directly towards me. He was dressed in a very simple white robe whose cape was thrown over the shoulder, giving the impression that he was walking against an invisible wind. Then my blood froze. I'd just noticed that this monk was wearing a crown of peacock feathers. I remembered having heard that the pope, instead of a jewel-encrusted tiara, wore this bizarre crown during ceremonies. Its symbolism expressed that his eyes, like those of the peacock feathers, were watching out in all directions to spot the birth of new heresies. It was the pope who was striding towards me now
.

For an instant I felt convinced that the pope knew who I was. I had time to wonder by what mystery he could have discerned his legate's murderer and to be astonished by the intelligence in his seemingly clairvoyant eyes. It was as if he were gazing at me with all the eyes of his peacock-feathered crown. I saw the spiral staircase that descends to the cells, the scalpel's lightning with which the executioners dissect and mentally consigned into the hands of God.

Then the pope stopped in his tracks and making the sign of the cross, with his thumb and first two fingers raised, he blessed me. It was then that I understood it was not Dalmas Rochemaure in particular that he was blessing, but that noisome jeering crowd gathered at my back which he was obliged to flatter and bless. Before I'd recovered from my surprise, he had crossed the church with his speedy step to lift the count of Toulouse by the shoulders and kiss him on both cheeks, calling him his dear son. I lifted the parchment, which he was going to need so badly, towards my master but he did not give me the sign that I was waiting for.

124

He was speaking to the pope with familiarity. He seemed fully at ease, abundantly expressing himself, his voice growing from strength to strength. I could only hear a few words, because of the distance, making out only a handful of scattered phrases. One name however took on an unexpected sonority on Innocent's lips and always reached me.

It was Pierre de Castelnau's name. So the bad man whom I had struck, for the evil he had done, was only dead in his material form. He was still very much alive for this pope, for his cardinals, for the great ecclesiastical sect for whom he had been a formidable champion. He was, if anything, living a more intense life and causing more evil now than when he existed in the flesh. It was to his memory that they had offered the holocaust of Béziers. He served as a pretext for vengeance for Simon de Montfort's massacres and the pillaging of Occitania. It was his name that Pope Innocent repeated with an irritated voice to the count of Toulouse as he knelt in penitence on the flagstones.

I had not reached the true source of evil. Beside the Rhône, in the morning twilight, I had only destroyed a simulacrum and multiplied the evil through my arrogant desire for revenge. The cause was not in the visible, material world but in the realm of the spiritual and the spirit had remained beyond my reach. Pierre de Castelnau would not cease his tormenting and killing and unearthing of the heretical dead. I thought that even now he stood at Pope Innocent's right hand. My soul's disorder was his doing. I remembered that the vapours that constitute the dead are dissolved by a steel blade and if I had had my sword I would have rushed to try and pierce that shadow.

Now, with a tremor in his voice, I heard the count glibly confessing. He said that he had done everything he could to try and bring Pierre de Castelnau's assassin to justice. He claimed that he was a good Christian and loved the church and defended her with all his power. Innocent's noble face filled with an indulgence of lies and before of their enemy's humiliation, the cardinals' eyes shone like cats. I was a witness to a ceremony of lies.

My master was lying for sure. He hated the Roman Catholic Church for its insolent tyranny, its insatiable thirst for riches and the evil with which it threatened him. He cherished the heretics and had made a Parfait swear to bring him the consolamentum* at the point of his death. He enumerated insignificant faults whilst omitting the pillage of abbeys, notably that of Saint-Gilles, which was, by the way, known to all. Pope Innocent lied too.

He had extended his hand to touch the count of Toulouse's forehead as if to grind him into oblivion only to grant him absolution instead but it was a false pardon. False too were the promises that he gave him now. He vowed to give him back the lands conquered by the crusaders when he had already irrevocably granted these lands to Simon de Montfort and even confirmed the donation to the legate's envoy. Now calling count Raymond his dear son, he was thinking of the city of Toulouse, queen of the realms of the Midi and heartland of the heretics. He was asking himself by which ruse he might dispossess the legitimate lord, whose skull he held in his hand.

In the empty space of the basilica, I saw the splendid city that sheltered the people of my race, with the red belt of its ramparts, with its steeples and flying buttresses, the flames in the houses and the radiance of its eternal soul. But this clairvoyant apparition only lasted a second. Grey clouds seemed to completely envelope it until only a blurred silhouette of Saint-Sernin remained in the middle of a woven fog of lies. Then the beautiful truth appeared to me. Truth was the most important thing in the world. The elect were those that lifted this living sword above the shadows where the inferior souls fought amongst themselves. I had killed Pierre de Castelnau, I had to proclaim that action, submit to the human consequences and lift towards the sun the hands that had spilt his blood. I felt oddly joyful, as one might feel arriving at the top of a mountain to discover an unlimited horizon. I took a step forward, filled my lungs with air and shouted as loud as I could:

"I killed Pierre de Castelnau!"

Somehow I didn't hear my voice resonating under the five arched naves of the Saint-Jean basilica. A wild clamor had just rung out around me and at the same time I was nudged then knocked over by a rain of gold coins.

I had vaguely perceived, through the blinding sincerity in which I was bathed, that a bureaucrat in violet, with crosses on his overcoat, had approached the count of Toulouse and murmured something in his ear. Once the pontifical ceremony was over, custom willed that the one, who had been received by the Holy Father, threw a large offering to the sovereign crowd. My master digging deep in his pockets had thrown the lot. Without fear for the majesty of the location or the presence under the altar of the embalmed heads of the apostles Peter and Paul, all the beggars in Rome had flung themselves onto their hands and knees, their shouts drowning my voice and causing my spirit to abruptly fall from the lofty heights where I had been gliding.

My forehead struck the bronze foot of the green basalt vessel where the emperor Constantine had bathed a few centuries earlier. When I got up the people, no doubt finding the offering too small, were proffering insults upon the count of Toulouse and Toulousans in general. From all corners I heard the word "heretic" pronounced with an Italian accent. The pope descended the master-altar, and with a familiar gesture he took with him his dear son, purified by repentance and absolution. The kneeling cardinals rose as one and it seemed as if the pillars were going to shatter, the vault explode with the secret force that emanated from their collective movement. They must have been accustomed to the crowd's jeers, as their faces expressed neither terror, nor disgust. Slowly, they peeled off in a circular line, stretching out like a serpent with a blood colored cardinal as every link. They disappeared through the side door to go and entwine themselves inside the earth.

Bruised and downhearted, I struggled to find my way amongst the unruly crowd. My whole life appeared in reverse to me, like one side of a medal whose other side would remain hidden forever.

I lived opposite to my soul's caricature and I would never see a soul in its true form for I could not even distinguish my own. With false joy the count of Toulouse showed me the ring enriched with an antique medallion that the pope* had given him.

"This ring must be worth fifty silver coins," he told me. "Actually, its value has no importance." He didn't stop looking at it and at length he respectfully kissed it. Then suddenly he let out a cry. He had just remembered the poison. He had some very old wine brought up and soaked the medallion ring in it for a long time. Then he asked God to forgive him this evil thought.

* The consolamentum was the Cathar last rites. Practiced by the Parfaits, it permitted the receiver to escape the chains of reincarnation.

* As well as the ring, the pope gave him a coat and a horse.

IX

If one could have gathered all the blood that had flowed from the wounds inflicted on my body throughout my life, it would fill a barrel big enough to hold a season's wine. Now, my body is full of scars like those big pine trees on the flanks of the Pyrénées that have been cut to let the resin flow. I spread my blood on the ramparts of every city subjected to the crusaders' sieges. On all the fields where the Southerners fought for the freedom of their country, I bled in vain, as my country was defeated. Toulouse was now under the authority of the king of France's seneschals and the pope's inquisitors. But I do not regret any of it for in futile courage, one finds a hidden virtue. The suffering of the oppressed is measured by a spiritual scale, where a small child's cry is heavier than a marching army and sooner or later the invisible balance re-establishes justice's equilibrium.

I took part in the defense of the château de Montréal and I was, I think, the only survivor for Simon de Montfort massacred every last soldier and inhabitant. Disguised as a peasant and helped by a few good men, I came by night and set fire to the war machines and the crusaders' tents as they camped under Carcassonne's ramparts. Beside Giraud de Pépieux, I defended Puysegur and I joined him in the assault on Montlaur. By Simon de Montfort's orders after the fall of Bram, all those who were captured had their eyes punctured and their noses cut off. Those villagers who had tried to remain hidden in their houses were rounded up and suffered the same horrific fate. I had disguised myself in a cassock and mixed with other monks in order to save my life. The holy brothers covered the victims' cries, by singing canticles. Luckily I remembered those canticles from my time in Mercus abbey.

When it came to the turn of a young girl, whose eyes looked like Esclarmonde's, it seemed that while trying to defend herself she held her arms out to me. My chanting became a horrific cry and all the monks turned their heads towards me. Some lucky stars protected one man from Bram. They only punctured one of his eyes, so that in the half-light of the other, he could lead the herd of blind ones to the fortress of Cabaret in order to teach its defenders that there was only darkness for those that resisted de Montfort.

In Minerve, when the square was taken I was amongst the eighty fighters, all knights and noblemen, that Simon de Montfort ordered to be hung so that they might die with ultimate humiliation. I found myself amongst Minerve's bravest with my hands tied behind my back, standing before the eighty gallows that had been constructed in haste.

All around me men groaned and cast insults at the crusaders. I was trying to resuscitate, in the depth of my soul, the figure of Esclarmonde de Foix, so that I might die with her image in my mind. Then suddenly I burst out laughing. Accompanied by a platoon of German soldiers, Simon de Montfort's wife, who had recently joined her husband, appeared in front of us, on a little hillock, to enjoy the eighty hangings of Minerve's vanquished. Her skin had a horribly yellow tint, the colour of the oil on the banks of the Rhône, the colour of Sicilian lemons. She was so prudish that she punished her servants when their skirts happened to lift, showing their anklebone. Leaning on the infamous scribe Pierre de Vaux-Cernay*, famous in the whole Christian world for his lies and the vileness of his writings, she rolled her beady eyes full of hate towards those who were about to die.

At the height of my mirth, I laughed so loudly that the good lord of Mercoriole, who had just been taken to be hung first, thought that I had lost my mind. I had pictured Simon de Montfort every evening under his tent next to this withered old vulture, this figure of hatred that was a veritable incarnation of hypocrisy.

I imagined the pious embrace between the warrior and that larva, dried up by her inner malignancy and I cracked up laughing. I praised God for his ability to chastise without it seeming so and thanked him for letting me die laughing with the knowledge of this chastisement.

However, the lord Mercoriole was very fat and his weight broke the newly prepared gallows. We realized that none of the gallows were particularly solid. Night was falling and they went off to announce this setback to Simon de Montfort, whose wife was getting impatient. Already someone was whispering that the execution would be postponed until tomorrow. Then Simon de Montfort sent the order to massacre all those that could not be hung by sword or lance. A certain confusion ensued. A lord with a loyal face was in charge of the executions but he was going about it in a detached way and I noticed that he was looking straight at me with unexpected sympathy. Was it because I had laughed and happiness wins certain hearts? He told a soldier to untie me and without a glance at de Montfort's wife, he pushed me towards the countryside.

In Lavaur I witnessed Guirande de Laurac's torment. Wounded, I had gone to her to seek refuge and I was healed by the Arab doctor Mohammed, who was a part of her court of wise men and poets.

I fought alongside the warrior queen for the thirty days of the siege and on the thirty third day, as the crusaders were mounting the final assault, the beautiful Guirande, lifting her crossbow to the sky, said some ambiguous words about us, whose interpretation threw me in a great muddle but I would never have the chance to penetrate the meaning. The town and the castle were taken and I owe my salvation to the Arab doctor with whom I developed an inspired friendship. De Montfort had only ignorant Northerners to treat his wounded, and with their salves and compresses they killed his men with a certain regularity. Mohammed's reputation must have preceded him for de Montfort ordered his life to be spared and he placed his guards around him and his remedies.

131

The excellent Mohammed threw an Arabic cloak around me and swore that I was his assistant, as expert as himself in the art of medicine.

We were taken out of the town to a field where they transported the crusaders who had fallen during the assault. It was there that, whilst pretending to be helping Mohammed, I saw them building a massive pyre where three hundred Parfaits were thrown and burned alive*.

From afar I saw Simon de Montfort, beside Alix, his young wife. His enormous stature, his massive forehead and hidden eyes made one think of an extraterrestrial being, unchained to destroy and cause suffering. I'd just pulled some water from a well to moisten a herbal cataplasm, when I saw the leader of the crusaders gesturing towards the well.

Two men were dragging Lavaur's queen on the end of a rope. Her hair was all over the place and a trickle of blood divided her face. She struggled to her feet, cursing them, when she discovered a spike had torn her dress, exposing her naked, palpitating breasts. Alix de Montfort made a gesture of disgust and turned to avoid seeing this flesh soiled with sin, or hearing her scandalous speech.

Then the men who held the rope lowered the queen of Lavaur into the well. For a long time I watched them throwing rocks and stones down after her. No cry came to my ears only a dull, thudding sound that eventually fell silent.

I saw other scenes too that were just as horrific, took part in other combats. I was often brave, sometimes cowardly but remained astonished at the huge love of life that creatures possess. I crossed villages where all the inhabitants had fled; I crossed the drawbridges of silent castles where my footsteps resonated in the empty halls and where the terror that had opened those doors still vibrated.

But one thing remained mysterious to me - Simon de Montfort was always victorious.

132

One could easily explain his constant victory by his personal courage, his luck, the number of his soldiers, the terror he inspired but I discerned another element. His victory seemed to have another cause, hidden in the very roots of destiny. It was inscribed in an unwritten book. In these times, in the too beautiful lands bordering the cerulean waters of the Garronne, evil was destined to triumph. Evil had incarnated in this man without pity. It was written that wherever his shadow fell, in the region where the philosophical poplar and the poetic fig once grew, the taste for beauty would be extinguished, along with songs that came from the heart, youth and intelligence. For ends that I didn't understand, my country, perfumed with Oriental amber, was to be ravaged by the hatred of that accursed one.

Now the mosaics of the beautiful fountains are shattered, marble statues no longer adorn the dwellings' thresholds, the semi-Arabic, semi-Roman towns have lost the turban of their turrets and the toga of their ramparts. But glory to that unnamed force by which a soul's properties are able to condense and sleep in a silent crucible in order to awake later! So, like the stratified plants that start living again with flowering petals and living stamens from the tap of a magical botanist's wand, so too the Occitan soul will resurrect.

* Pierre de Vaux-Cernay accompanied Simon de Montfort and was the historian indignantly partial to the crusade.

* Pierre de Vaux-Cernay recalls in his chronicles that they were burned "with great joy". One does not know for sure if he was talking about the crusaders' great joy, or that which the Albigensians showed in shedding their earthly life.

Part Three

I

My sister Aude had become the most charming young girl in Toulouse. Her beauty didn't grab you, but it grew on you in the same way that a landscape, blessed with delicate measures of colour, takes a certain presence to conceive its poetic beauty.

It was a great pleasure to spend time with her on my return to Toulouse, after years of absence. The count Raymond had passed this time in vain negotiations, petitioning the legates. He had been humiliated and deceived. Finally deciding to split from the church and Simon de Montfort, he offered and I resumed my position beside him.

I had the gift of making my sister Aude laugh. She found totally ordinary things took on a comedic aspect when they came out of my mouth. This wasn't a mockery; it was a way of sharing affection, as certain captive birds sing when approached. Strangely enough there was a mysterious bond between my sister Aude and our feathered friends. She walked so lightly that she often appeared to be flying. Leaning on her windowsill overlooking Saint-Sernin, she would continually repeat the same sound, changing its modulation until she had fallen into a kind of ecstasy. I noticed that her eyes became a blue-violet colour that I had only once seen in a lost lake in the Pyrénées.

Aude had been instructed in the Albigensian faith and she could hold forth on the philosophy of this religion. She tried a few times to explain it to me and what she said was always very beautiful, but all too often incomprehensible. She told me everything that happens to creatures after their death, going into the smallest details. I wondered how she had come to know such things that were so far out of our common knowledge. I learned from her that all the bad one does to another followed a mystical curve, coming back to strike you in exactly the same way. The curve was sometimes very long and when it could not reach you in this life, it would catch up with you in the next.

Aude promised me that I'd already lived and that I would live again to receive the good and the evil that I had done. I asked her that if a man who had pierced another man's chest with a lance, having meditated upon his action all night, would he for sure be struck in the same way, in his own chest. She laughed as usual, not suspecting that it was me that I was talking about. She went on to assure me that that man would surely die a violent death, as he was no doubt stupid and loveless. There was, however, a way, and a practice to avoid these reincarnations and such heavy retribution was not always inevitable. Few were able to understand these practices, as it required such a pure heart.

Initially, I was proud of the love Aude had for me. I realized however that she had an extraordinary love not only for her Mother and Father, but also her friends, her dog, the austere Albigensians with whom she had meetings and even those who passed in the street that she had never met. When you said to her: "it's cold", she began weeping for all the creatures that would die in the fields. When the sun was setting, one could see red spots on her forehead from the mosquitoes she refused to kill. She would never admit it for fear of being ridiculed. When we went for a walk, I observed her scrupulously making sure not to squash a blade of grass on the path. Aude was often sad and I asked her why.

135

"I would like," she told me, "to accomplish a really good deed and I can't."

I reminded her that she gave all her money to the poor and even devoted her life to them. The day before, the executioner, Tancrede, the most evil man in the city, had almost been knocked out in a street near our house. All the doors had shut, everyone willing his death, only Aude had run out to bandage his wound and for that she had received only curses as thanks.

"All good deeds bring joy when they are accomplished, and because of that they are not terribly desirable. It is only in suffering that one becomes pure. I want to accomplish a good deed that brings me pain."

�֎

A runner carried a vine branch announcing the arrival of the new wine when I met the monk Petrus in a bar near the Bazacle gate. We went and sat together under a gazebo. "You've become an unholy dog of a heretic," he said jovially. I no longer remember with what insults I answered him, but it was about the bishop Foulque, because Petrus had become his most fanatical servant. Under his orders, he organized some gangs that were called the "Whites". The members recognized each other by the white shirts they wore. They gathered with the sole aim of pillaging the houses belonging to heretics. Since my arrival I'd been meaning to organize a rival gang that would be called "the Blacks", who would rally around my black leather surcot. I saw the hatred emanate from his being and it seemed to me for an instant that a wild black dog was prowling around us. He lowered his voice and told me, as if it were a secret one could only tell a friend:

"Toulouse is doomed! Her destruction has been decided. She can no longer avoid it."

I asked him with the softness that Aude always incited me to observe, who had decided this destruction. He wanted to intimidate me and pointed right next to where I was sitting.

"Look at that peasant," he said but there was no one next to me.
"Well?" I answered.
"It's Jesus Christ," he murmured with false respect. "I see him almost everyday. He's the one who told me about Toulouse's destruction."

I drew my sword, with the composure prescribed by Aude and drew a cross with the tip of the blade on the place where the beggar was supposedly sitting. Then, with a shrug of the shoulders I let Petrus know that he was not fooling me. He clenched his teeth. His fists were tight. He told me:

"It's bishop Foulque who decided it. The "Whites" whom I command have divided the city into quarters. When the time comes we will set it on fire." I internally invoked God to dominate me and surprisingly succeeded. I even promised myself to tell Aude about this victory over my natural violence. My smile exasperated Petrus and in his rage he snapped at me:

"Your house too will be burned. You will be spared because you are my friend. But as for your sister Aude, we have waited a long time to have her. She is so popular, we had to draw lots and I am the lucky winner!" The universe around me turned red and as his last syllable was still resonating, I struck his face with my dagger. I wonder how he didn't die from such a stroke. No doubt a movement he made saved his life. Blood poured from his left eye that had burst.

I heard him calling for any "Whites" who may have been in the neighbourhood. I felt strong enough to take on a whole army. I tipped over the table to make a barricade but no one came.

It was in this way that friendships ended in the times we lived.

That evening, without telling her what had happened, I asked Aude if someone, during a conversation with his friend happened to burst his eye in a moment of violence, would they then in turn have their own eye burst in a future life? She contented herself by saying:

"Would it not be justice?" I answered her that in effect it would be justice. I then thought of all the arrows I had shot, all the blows I had given in battle, and it seemed to me that the surface area of my body would never be sufficient to carry all the wounds that I had given.

I had pity on the poor creature that I was and thus prepared for my martyrdom.

II

The battle of Muret* was over. The king of Aragon was dead and his army had dispersed. Simon de Montfort could force Toulouse's gates at any moment. A catastrophic breath hung over the city. To make matters worse, the annual plague that struck the poorer neighborhoods was taking more victims than usual.

I pleaded with my parents to get out and go to a piece of land one of my uncles owned near Rabastens. My father refused. Anyway, Aude was incapable of making even the smallest journey. Since the fighting had started around Toulouse she had become extremely feeble. Her body was constantly twitching, as if she was feeling every blow on the battlefields. She never stopped praying.

The count Raymond decided to leave the city before the roads to the North were blocked by de Montfort's troops. A huge entourage of knights and cavalry rode with him.

The horses and bags were all ready and waiting at the Matabiau gate. The moon was rising on the clay roofs and Saracen towers. I met the count in his garden. Walking up the central alley, I was surrounded by a whirlwind of wings. All the aviaries were open but the birds, instead of profiting from their freedom, were perched on the lower branches of the surrounding trees as if they were waiting for something. The count was immobile, next to his favorite swan and from afar, under the moonlight, he looked like the bizarre and desperate lord of some bird people.

He didn't know what to do. The swan that he loved did not want to leave him.

No doubt she understood the gravity of the situation for she refused to be caught, yet would not leave his side. He feared abandoning her and he couldn't leave at the head of an army with a swan in his arms! He added that he preferred knowing that she was dead, rather than abandoning her and he ordered me to kill her as quickly as I could.

I never had the chance to execute this unpleasant task. I'd barely taken a step towards the swan when, by a massive coincidence or a mysterious comprehension, she flew off over the garden, over the houses to God knows where. The count signaled me to follow him. We crossed roads filled with silent cavalrymen, all heading towards the Matabiau gate. We reached the bridge over the Garonne and came to Saint-Cyprien, the neighborhood most affected by the plague. Many of the houses looked abandoned and the two or three glimmers of light we saw in the windows, were candles watching over the dead. In a road that ran along a wall we stopped in front of a convent door.

There were two crests hanging on this door. I recognized the count's golden cross on a black key. Four of his guards were sitting a little further on. The count looked at the second crest with surprise and his mood darkened.

He knocked on the convent door. It took a long time before it was opened. An old toothless woman, holding a candle, screamed and almost fell over when she saw us. Toothlessness is chief among the cosmic insults heaped upon mankind and accordingly we could barely understand a word of what she was trying to tell us. I thought I made out that the plague had taken several lives in the convent and all the nuns had fled. However someone must have remained behind as the old lady walked off down a stone walled gallery and the count followed her without hesitation, as if he knew the way.

We stopped in front of a door that was ajar and from which a soft light emanated. With her long hand the woman opened the door then stood aside immediately.

Four candles lit the room, indicating by their geometry that whomsoever they were illuminating was dead.

I saw a skeletal silhouette, a face that had kept a grotesque smile under tangled white hair. Madness, stronger than death, still left its mark. A man was kneeling in the corner of the room. Without getting up he glanced over and his gaze crossed the count's, who went and knelt beside him. I recognized Arnaud Bernard.

I was a witness to the last scene in the drama that, thirty years ago, had shaken Toulouse. Alix Bernard had loved the count Raymond so much that it had driven her mad and she had been kept in this convent in Saint-Cyprien ever since. Now, the two men who had unequally shared her love were kneeling beside her body from whence all signs of beauty had fled. They came in spite of the dangers that were besieging the city, attempting to save the symbol of their undying youth. The two faithful old men were side by side, united in the same prayer but Arnaud Bernard took his tardy revenge. The final rights belonged to him, the last good-bye next to the coffin. The count no doubt understood. He got up, suddenly timid, backed away and left with his head bowed.

When we were in the road, he asked me if I knew what happened to mad people's souls after death and if they found their reason again. I answered that I had no idea, but that I wouldn't forget to question my sister on the subject.

❖

* The king of Aragon had come to the count of Toulouse's rescue with a sizeable army. They attacked Simon de Montfort near Muret. It was there that the fate of the Midi was decided.

III

Soldiers lead by a man with a hideously ugly square head were gathering around the town hall. I thought I was living in a nightmare. The people of Toulouse were gathered and waiting. Opposite me, in the middle of the crowd, I could see Petrus surrounded by a troop of armed "Whites". His one eye shone like a terrible lamp.

All of a sudden there was a murmur, a whispering of voices, followed by a crushing silence. A magnificently dressed person appeared on the threshold of the town hall, holding a large parchment from which shining seals hung. He glanced nervously at the windows opposite him and I realized he was little more than a cowardly clerk. He unfolded the parchment with trembling hands and started reading with a hollow voice, uniquely preoccupied by thoughts of the arrow of justice that could spring forth from any window at any moment. What he read, in a stony silence, started like this:

"Philippe, by the grace of God, king of France, to all his friends and vassals. Know that we have received our dear and loyal Simon de Montfort as the duke of Narbonne, count of Toulouse*..."

I only heard so much. The rest was only one of those official and incomprehensible formulas by which the rich like to express themselves on parchments.

My master Raymond VI was dispossessed of his city and his estates. When the clerk was finished, the despoiler left the town hall and stopped a moment on the steps.

142

His square head wobbled as a sign of respect in front of bishop Foulque, who then followed him. Foulque seemed prodigiously fat and I thought it might be due to the several coats of chain mail he was wearing under his priestly gowns. His hands were covering his face, pretending to be hiding tears. I knew, thanks to Sezelia, that the pepper stuffed under his nails produced them. Behind them came Guy de Montfort, Simon's brother and the horrible Alix, wearing a dress sparkling with stolen jewellery. Other despoilers and other bishops followed.

The Capitouls appeared last. They seemed to have difficulty breathing, no doubt due to their burning tongues, having just sworn their sermon of obedience to their new lord. I also thought I noticed their right hands were sore, due to the signature by which they confirmed their sermon. Bernard de Colomies no longer wore jewellery, Etienne Carabordes, the greengrocer, had become skinny. Pons Barbadal the wine merchant had lost his colour. As the doomed walked in the middle of the soldiers, I remembered what Petrus had told me not long ago and also what Sezelia had spoken of. Toulouse's destruction was imminent. The man covered in iron and the man who wore a mitre were incarnations of evil as prophesied by the enlightened Marie. It was because of the prophetic words of this seer that the third member of this infernal trinity had had his body's dust thrown to the wind. And so the prophecy was realized.

That evening I barricaded my front door and put a crossbow by each window. Several times, looking up the rue du Taur, I thought I saw Petrus' shining eye.

⛬

I shared my worries with Aude and she told me that prayer could right even the greatest wrongs, if the one praying consented to bring these wrongs upon themselves. During the night, through the wall that separated our bedrooms, I heard her repeating:

143

"May all of Toulouse's suffering come into my body and my soul!" I couldn't believe such a thing possible, but nevertheless found it imprudent not to try. I often begged my sister to stop, but always in vain.

Toulouse's destruction had started. Many of the palaces in the center of town were fortified. Simon de Montfort ordered that their towers be dismantled, lest they be used as a refuge, in the event of a riot. The chains in the roads were removed so that the German cavalry could sweep through without obstruction and hundreds of workers attacked the ramparts. But these ramparts built in part with Arnaud Bernard's knowledge of stone, were prodigious cyclopean monuments. They had to be content with merely creating a few holes.

I perceived with horror that the continuous prayer that Aude had undertaken, had begun to show. A mysterious link had established itself between her and the city. When they started destroying the Commenges tower, she developed a strange wound on her shoulder. When the queen of towers had her pink granite crown removed, part of which still dominates the Sardine gate, some kind of bloody ring formed around her forehead. Sometimes, she called me at the break of dawn. She knew by a pain in her body that somewhere a new demolition had begun.

Everything that happened at the Macaroon tower echoed in her throat. The fall of the Basacle fortress was inscribed in her hands. In her heart she felt the tower of Saint-Rhemesy coming down. I ended up completely believing that my sister's life was linked to Toulouse. When I begged her to stop the prayer that she pursued internally, she answered me:

"The sacrifice I'm making isn't a real sacrifice, since I'm happy making it." I will not dwell on the terrible years that followed. My mother died. My father was one of the eighty hostages Simon de Montfort demanded from the people of Toulouse after the first revolt. He massacred them under a false pretext.

With Arnaud Bernard and a few valiant men I went from house to house collecting the thirty thousand marcs that Simon de Montfort demanded after the second revolt in order to save Toulouse from pillage.

Chance favored me the night Petrus, accompanied by two of his companions jumped into my garden, with the intention of taking Aude. I killed all three before they had the chance to cry out and I buried them at the foot of a laurel. I don't know if they sleep in peace. The laurel carried on growing. Chance was contrary the night when, on my stomach on a rooftop, I shot an arrow at Simon de Montfort. He stood under the porch the moment he left Saint-Etienne. Barely fifty meters separated us. A hidden force deflected the arrow, as the time had not yet come.

When every inhabitant, under pain of death, left in front of their door, all the weapons in their possession I organized workshops in cellars where we forged new swords and carved wooden lances. During the third riot, I was amongst those who pushed Simon de Montfort and his army back into the Narbonnais castle. I was then delegated with six others to stand, humiliated before him. Kneeling, we could hear bishop Foulque pleading with de Montfort to kill us. His face wasn't covered with a hypocritical mask and his nails needed no tear-inducing pepper. He let his hatred plainly show. The seven men kneeling before him were nothing to him. What he wanted was the death of the heretical city. He explained this necessity with eloquence. He swore that God wanted this sacrifice and even inspired it*.

While he was talking, I heard a light vibration in the air, a sound that was seemingly produced by nothing and which was also that note sometimes mysteriously modulated by Aude, when she fell into ecstasy. Was it her prayer, which by some secret magic, penetrated the hall and influenced the perpetrators of evil? The troops that were amassing on the squares and crossroads waiting for the order to break into the houses and start pillaging were suddenly given orders to leave the city.

The seven ambassadors of Toulouse came out of the Narbonnais castle, stupefied to be alive.

There were nights when Aude lost her breath and I thought she was about to die. I looked out of the window to watch for the glow of the fire that the Whites were wishing for. I stabbed a man who had piled up dry twigs against the door of the Roaix family and was approaching it with lit tinder. Another time, in the Saint-Sernin cemetery I heard noises that were coming from under ground and I never found out whether it was the dead waking or miners sent by Foulque to undermine the church. Nevertheless Aude got better and Toulouse survived or vice versa. Simon de Montfort left the city with his cavalry to go warmongering in the Rhône valley. The monuments dug their foundations even deeper into the ancient soil. It seemed that the dismantled towers took root. I thought I noticed the ramparts expanding. The Dalbade bell tower even grew a few meters in height.

Then, one sunny September day, my sister Aude went down into the garden for the first time in ages and picked a bouquet of flowers. Soon after a strange phenomenon entered the city. The thickest fog ever seen fell on its walls, perhaps to hide what was going to happen to de Montfort's soldiers and the traitors. This fog spread a denser veil over the part of the Garonne that flows at the extremity of Toulouse, around the Basacle ford. It is by this ford that around five o'clock in the evening the count Raymond VI, still the lord of Toulouse in the Toulousans' hearts, crossed the Garonne, with Roger Bernard de Foix on his right and Bernard de Commenges on his left and behind him some valiant and invincible men.

Up to my knees in water I was the first to take his horse's bridle and to tell him what had to be told. While Etienne Carabordes and Pons Barbadal cried with emotion and Pierre de Roaix shouted inarticulate shrieks, because of his tongue that had been ripped out at the Narbonnais castle for speaking ill of God. As the Basacle doors were being opened I seized a bugle and as a joke with a formidable lung-full, I blew the call to arms.

146

From this resonance, the two hundred thousand inhabitants of Toulouse appeared in the same second at their windows, while underneath them the foundations of their houses flinched, regaining the immortality of their stones.

At the sound of the bugle Alix de Montfort scarpered for refuge in the Narbonnais* castle with the few soldiers who had escaped the Toulousan fury. She had all four drawbridges raised, her teeth rattling in terror.

That evening, as I wandered in the city, I heard on the cross roads, in the doorways and in the bars, all the people were talking about Alix de Montfort's nose. For it was mighty long and disgraceful. Everyone maintained having seen it out of a window in the Eagles tower, disproportionately elongated.

* This is the start of the charter of investiture that Philippe-Auguste signed in June 1216 in Melun. Simon de Montfort was recognized by him as duke of Narbonne, count of Toulouse, viscount of Béziers and Carcassonne.

* Simon de Montfort had agreed to Fouquet's wishes and was going to destroy Toulouse, which numbered more inhabitants than today. It was his brother Guy and a few of his barons who dissuaded him.

* The Narbonnais castle was not situated in the city centre, but outside of the ramparts.

IV

Delga du Lauragais requested the Baziège gate. He maintained that it would make him fight better as in fair weather he could see the village where he was born. The brave Palauqui de Foix had chosen Saint-Cyprien as his post because it was the spot closest to the Pyrénées, from which he could feel the forest's breath. The lord of Montaut commanded the Basacle gate and the lord of Pailhas the Sardane gate. Arnaud Bernard took the Villeneuve gate as it was there that the biggest gash had been made in the ramparts and because it was the most dangerous post.

Emeric de Rocanaga, the scholar, was at the Gaillarde gate. A servant endlessly followed him with his philosophy books. He had terrible eyesight and he insisted to be read to, even when he stood on the ramparts amidst a rain of arrows. He maintained that the reading of Plato made for a wonderful shield. The reading clerk was not of this opinion and sometimes lost his voice. It happened that an arrow pierced right through a manuscript. The lord of Rocanaga was thrilled as he saw a deeper meaning in it, Aristotle having recently replaced Plato.

At the old bridge's barbican the astronomer Sicard de Puylaurens was in command. He knew, through his studies of the heavens, everyone's date of death but he kept it to himself saying that such knowledge was dangerous. He was extremely careful for someone who knew that he was going to live another forty years. He had no doubt made a few mistakes in his calculations as he drowned a few days later in the Garonne during a moonlit swim.

The young Dor de Barsac and Guillaume de Balafar rendered the Pertus barbican invincible by their presence.

Bertrand de Pestillac, the magnificent, was at the Montolieu gate. He wore a jersey over his breastplate embroidered with pearls and he was so covered in jewels, ornaments and panache that he looked like one of those Spanish saints, who fold in the gold of their reliquary, the richness of their votive offering. I was positioned at the Matabiau gate with Frederic de Frezols, the pious one. His prayer was so deep that, once in, no alarm bell or trumpet could pull him out. He said that God was watching out for him. I was given the responsibility to take command when he knelt down, because God might be a poor look out, especially as he apparently favoured the other side.

In all the towers and on all the gates were men both admirable and fearless but it was beside Saint-Sernin, in the rue du Taur, within my sister's breast that Toulouse's heart beat.

For nine months Simon de Montfort attacked the city from all sides at once. He had received huge reinforcements from France. He had built a massive machine of war that we called 'Goliath' and he dominated all of our towers with this rolling monster. The terror he inspired was heightened by the prospect of the reprisals he would inevitably exert if he once more became master of the city. As the terror grew, so did our desire to be rid of him and this desire took root in count Raymond. During his whole life the count had shown a certain aversion to combat and his lack of heroism was well known, yet for no apparent reason the people had begun to consider him to be one of the most valiant warriors to stand against the infernal legions of Christianity. This spontaneously spreading belief had even won the count's heart. We had to beg him not to be too rash. He wanted to challenge Simon de Montfort in single combat and he had no doubt who would be the winner of such a nonsensical combat.

This conception of his worth, that everyone shared had brought his youth back. He stood taller. He asked me to buy him some cosmetics for his moustache. For many years now he had been called "old Raymond." He let me know that it was his enemies who had given him the ridiculous nickname. He felt younger than his son. He claimed that his strength was increasing daily. He was thinking of getting married again, for the sixth time.

He nearly cried with happiness when an old lady, seeing him pass in the street, shouted out:

"It's the archangel Michael!" In reality a rejuvenation had spread throughout Toulouse, as if the city's freedom quickened our blood.

Pierre Carabordes, in spite of his large stomach, had taken up running so that he might all the better chase the enemy at the next opportunity. We saw him pass, naked to the waist, dripping in sweat and wagging his black stick on the path around the ramparts. Pons Barbadal maintained that singing had such a big influence on courage that he had created a choir out of the militia of commanders in front of Saint-Sernin. The quadrilateral of Arnaud Bernard's face was rounding due to the joy he was feeling as he looked over the rebuilt towers and ramparts. He had cockily left the Villeneuve gate open. His soldiers with helmets and breastplates were positioned five in line, the first of which were kneeling and shooting crossbows and the last dominated the others by their taller stature. This phalanx was as wide as the gate and the length of the lances were proportioned to the position the fighters took. The phalanx moved forward and backward with a signal but it never exceeded the cities fortifications. It was like a living gate, bristling with steel, on which hundreds of horses and men came and perished, but which remained more inexorably shut than bronze or stone.

However, when the tenth month of the siege had come, it appeared to even the most judicious spirits that the situation was hopeless. The circumference of the ramparts was so large that the fighters couldn't move swiftly enough to the areas under attack.

To make matters worse, Simon de Montfort had stepped up his unexpected attacks. The chains that had been stretched across the river had stopped the supplies that the count's of Foix and Comminges were sending by boat on the Garonne. The archers from Bordeaux that Arcis de Montesquieu had introduced began to get discouraged.

⁕

I remember that morning, there was such a delicate tint of orange in the sky that Aude pointed it out with the end of her little finger, showing me that it was the same color as her dress.

I was off to the Saint-Sernin gate and my sister followed. She had a resolute air about her and she told me she had decided she would also participate in the city's defence. Nearly all the women of Toulouse, under the orders of the dame de Roaix, spent their days at the ramparts, repairing weapons, supplying arrows or stones and tending to the wounded. Dame de Roaix wore a breastplate and sword and even took part in the sorties.

I tried to dissuade Aude from coming with me. She fainted from the mere touch of a sword. She was so weak she couldn't even draw a crossbow for someone. She could be of no help but Aude shook her head and she started walking by my side, with a firm stride, in her orange-sky coloured dress. She was walking faster than me now and I noticed something strange about her. Maybe, I thought, she had had a dream that night foretelling my death. I remembered having a dream that might have been interpreted in that way and perhaps she wanted to be there for my last moments. I was touched by the effort she was making but felt sorry for myself.

Around Saint-Sernin, some armed men came running. They shouted that the Montolieu gate was being attacked.

151

I recognized Ratier de Caussade, the runner, who was in charge of gathering all the available soldiers and leading them toward the thick of the onslaught.

My orders were to stay on the Saint-Sernin gate, whatever happened. I was relieved. The spot my sister would spend the day was going to be out of the battle, as it was obviously happening at Montolieu that day. I led her by a spiral staircase to the rooftops of Saint-Sernin's old cloisters. It was half demolished but the part of roof that remained stood above the ramparts and we had installed all sorts of catapults and trebuchets, several of which were invented by Bernard Paraire and could throw blocks of a daunting size. There were normally some women Aude knew up there.

I was laughing as I climbed the stairs saying to myself: "Dreams and presentiments are a fiction of vanity."

From this cloister's roof we dominated the devastated countryside. Frederic de Frezols had been in command of the Saint-Sernin gate the whole night and normally went off to sleep when I arrived. He hadn't waited for me that morning. He was kneeling; his hands together and the fervour of his prayer had tipped him into a deep sleep. As I looked into the distance I saw a layer of dust strangely lined the horizon but the air around me was still. What was that strange wind that wouldn't let Toulouse feel it? Then I heard the tremor of an enormous stampede and an instant later a trumpet burst out underneath me. Voices cried out:

"There they are!" Lord de Frezols woke up and started running around giving incoherent orders. Then, all of a sudden, I remembered that I had only brought a visor-less helmet. It was too late to go and change it. Death would surely strike me in the face, no doubt by the intermediary of an arrow.

The countryside was now covered in cavalry. They had slowed their pace, but we could hear their horses neighing and see their weapons gleaming. The attack on Montolieu was a bluff.

The entire army was getting ready to strike Saint-Sernin with a massive military mallet. I shouted for the mangonels to be manned in the hope of stopping the enemy under an avalanche of stones.

By my count there were no more than fifty archers on this part of the ramparts.

Then the shouts fell silent and all eyes turned towards the enemy. Simon de Montfort had just peeled off from the front line of his cavalry. He knew the terror his sight produced and always made sure it was a theatrical appearance. The clear sun made his helmet, his shield and everything right down to his spurs shine, so that from head to foot he seemed filled with light. His upraised sword was like a supernatural beam by which he communicated with the sun.

I saw, as if in a dream, people stumbling over each other.

Two men had just hitched up the tourniquet of the largest of the trebuchets. A dwarf, shouting to increase his zeal, was struggling with a basket overflowing with stones. I recognized that these stones were fragments of smashed statues. Bishop Foulque had, the previous year, ordered all the pagan statues on the houses to be torn down. He had solemnly exorcised the pieces in front of Saint-Sernin and there they had stayed, stacked up in a corner of the cemetery. We had been using them for a couple of days to load the bricoles. I recognized the head of Minerva in the basket. She seemed to be looking right at me and I marveled realising that the head resembled Esclarmonde de Foix. A decapitated Esclarmonde de Foix lay in a dwarf's basket.

"Sign of the times!" I told myself. The dwarf took the Minerva head and put it in the leather pouch of the closest mangonel. The rope was tight and even though it was a small mangonel the dwarf's efforts at loosening it were futile. As the thoughts rushed into my mind, with the ardour that Toulousans show when attacking their enemy, I thought about Ulysses and his divine bow. But the dwarf let out a scream.

An arrow had just pierced his ear and entered his neck at an angle. He fell and remained sitting in the stream of his blood.

Then, out of the blue, my sister Aude took a step forward, grabbed the mangonel's rope and loosened it with a single movement full of ease, sending Minerva's head, Esclarmonde's head across the sunlit space.

I did not see the arc of this predestined stone but an enormous clamour let me know towards whom its wise and inexorable destiny had lead it. In the middle of the spluttering rays, the luminary knight, the leader of evil, the despot's headless body, remained upright on his horse a second more. Then he collapsed on this Toulousan earth that he hated and where he had caused so much suffering.

"Simon de Montfort's dead!" Shouted a voice that seemed to come out of the Saint-Sernin basilica.

"He's dead!" Shouted the ramparts. "He's dead!" shouted the city.

By several gates the Toulousans rushed out. An enchantment had been broken; a diabolic magic had just been brought to an end by a stone thrown by an innocent hand. It appeared that the evil power, when struck at its source crumbled and seemed to dissolve, as if it were made of nothing. The immense army, which surrounded Toulouse, beat a hasty retreat and we heard the departing monks singing funereal hymns around their headless warrior.

That evening, worn out by a day's fighting but relieved that no arrow had struck my face; I came back to the Saint-Sernin gate and climbed to the abbey's roof. Tents were still burning in the distance, throwing up uncertain flames. On my right, the skeleton of the Gate smoked and was falling apart piece by piece. The dead made calm little humps. A mad horse turned in a circle and sometimes reared up on its hind legs. A breastplate shone like a forgotten sun. In a burned wheat field a tall and skinny man was running.

154

He had his hands tied behind his back and a sword stuck in his chest. No doubt one of de Montfort's men had struck the prisoner before running away.

He ran with what was left of his strength, in order to die amongst his brothers, a symbol of the martyred city, eternally living, in spite of the wound in the heart of her stones.

❁

* A chronicler at the time wrote that de Montfort's head was ripped clean off his shoulders by the stone.

V

Aude died. At least she died according to the common conception of death. One day, her heart stopped beating and then she stopped breathing. Standing next to her, I understood for the first time that such a phenomenon really shouldn't be called death.

Aude had never managed to forgive herself for having let loose that almighty stone.

"I finally accomplished a good deed that makes me suffer," she said with a sad smile. She became silent, attentive to voices and signs that she was alone to understand. When she was sure that life was about to leave her body she became unusually happy. She spent her last days waiting for the light that would lead her away. It reminded me of my youth when I waited to be taken to the countryside with my uncle from Rabastens. I was alone to hear her last words, as Aude didn't want anyone's last rights.

"May he forgive me for having taken his life, as one day all those he put to death will forgive him." Improbable wish, I thought through my tears.

I was tempted to follow my sister into that soft world which drew its beauty from the absence of all forms of sensation. However life was solidly attached to my body by its carnal roots. I was resolved to study the Albigensian religion and to force myself to become as pure as she prescribed. I went to find Frédéric de Roaix, the Capitoul's brother, who had once taken me to a heretical reunion where I had heard people speaking of the Holy Ghost.

I told him that I aspired for a higher knowledge than the ordinary man possessed and added that I thought I had become wiser than I had been in the past. At first it looked as if he didn't believe me then he told me that I was a brave man full of courage and I had nothing to worry about. I insisted and eventually he accepted to give me the instruction I was asking for, but like all people who deal in subtle things, he did so in a willfully complicated language. I asked him several times if he couldn't explain himself a bit clearer. He smiled and I understood that he was making a real effort not to tell the cretin that I was to stop wasting his time. I remain convinced however that he could have expressed himself in simpler words.

I understood that there was a primitive teaching brought back by Bartholomew, the apostle who was sent on an evangelical mission to Persia and India. Bartholomew, in these distant lands ended up being instructed rather than instructing. He returned to Hieropolis in Phrygia and there, still evangelizing, he gave a teaching that on many points was very different from Jesus'*. His disciples, struck by the beaming strength of truth, had collected his words and transmitted them in secrecy, as they held a substance contrary to all human society.

Life is bad, in its essence and one must destroy the force of desire that everyone carries, which is the root of all evil. The strength of this desire rushes us, after our death, into another earthly reincarnation and this race through human forms is without end if we do not discover the secret by which we can reach the beatitude of perfect intelligence. This secret is revealed to one who reaches the Holy Ghost, the divine wisdom. Then, the race ends and man enters through love into God's serenity. I was touched by the truth of these things, but couldn't repress a great sadness at the condemnation of life. The sparkling sun, womanly shapes and Toulouse's stones continued to enchant me. Sitting in my garden, meditating on the Sofia of the Parfaits, I was watching a bee landing on a fruit, a branch moving in the wind, the shadow of a bird passing across a row of vegetables and I was remorseful in finding something charming about the perishable beauty of these images.

I only understood much later that the bee, the bird's shadow, the moving branch are even more beautiful when one has arrived through detachment to the fullness of love.

⚜

One evening towards five o'clock, a messenger came to me on behalf of the count, who had recently knighted me and now treated me as an equal. Many evenings I would take council with him and a certain Hugues Jean, whom he loved for his great simplicity, and who lived in a house in the suburb behind Saint-Sernin.

The count must have been waiting impatiently for me, for I saw him making signs at me from the first floor window. While I was climbing the staircase, the count had one of his attacks that are common for older folk. The moment I opened the door he fell into a chair.

"You took such a long time." Hugues Jean told me. "The count of Toulouse was waiting for you so that he could inform us both of something of great importance." When I saw the count I understood that he was about to die. It did seem like he had something urgent to say, but had unfortunately been struck by a paralytic immobility that only allowed him to emit inarticulate sounds. Only his feet were moving. Then they stopped as well. His expression was one of formidable desire. Hugues Jean and I were of the same opinion. His desire concerned some form of religious help. But which one? He no doubt wanted to confess. But to whom? For years the count of Toulouse had been accompanied everywhere by the Albigensian Parfait, Bertrand Martin. He had often said to his familiars that he adhered to the new religion from the bottom of his heart. When he was ill, he said:

"Go quickly and find Bertrand Marty."

158

On the other hand, he had recently been to confession with some catholic priests and he had secretly taken communion at the church of the Daurade. Numerous excommunications' weighed on him, but the priests had closed their eyes. A few months before, bishop Foulque had returned to Toulouse and the count had been forced to accept him. The bishop made a point of reminding the people that the excommunication that weighed on the count could only be lifted by the pope. He had promised to write in his favour. As time passed the count had, once again, got Bertrand Marty to come around. What was he requesting now from his twisted and silent lips?

"It doesn't matter, it's all the same God," Hugues Jean told me in a hushed voice. He was a sensible but rather vulgar man.

I laid my master on a bed that was at the end of the room. His terrified and begging expression overwhelmed me with pity. I regretted not being a priest so that I could give him the absolution and the peace he was asking for. I even thought about swearing on Jesus-Christ that I had secretly become a Parfait and then giving him a simulacrum of the consolamentum.

I had time for nothing. There were noises in the house and the door burst open. I saw the abbot of Saint-Sernin appear as he was followed by several of his canons that were still filing up the staircase. This abbot had recently returned to Toulouse with bishop Foulque. He was a hard-hearted man with a face like a bad omen. No doubt some servants had prematurely announced the count's death. I assumed that his immobility confirmed it, as the abbot barely cast a look his way. He said with a severe voice:

"The body of the count of Toulouse belongs to Saint- Sernin abbey." I leaned over and whispered:

"But, thank God! Our lord the count is not dead. He's merely paralyzed!" From the corner of my eye, I could see my master was making an enormous effort to regain his speech.

159

Instead of checking what I had said the abbot of Saint-Sernin stepped back with disgust and said, turning to his canons:

"Get this miserable heretic out of here. His presence is a stain next to the body of our lord Raymond." I neither had the time, nor the desire, to express what was comic about asking his canons to force me to leave.

"The count is alive," I said as I turned towards these stone figures. Then the staircase erupted and pushing pass the canons were several knights of the Order of Saint-Jean de Jerusalem, who stormed into the room.

"The count's body belongs to Saint-Sernin," claimed the abbot with a peremptory voice.

"It belongs to the Order," answered the Order's priest in a thundering voice.

The count Raymond was narrowly linked to the knights of Malta as he had made them responsible for his alms. He had confided his last testament to them and may even have asked them to bury him. This deed entailed some precious privileges. For three days the community that carried it out would receive all sorts of offerings.

"The count is not dead!", I shouted with all my strength, but the tumult covered my voice. The Order's priest took off his white coat, adorned with a golden cross, and threw it on the bed as a sign of possession. The coat was heavy, and I thought that my master might suffocate under it. The abbot of Saint-Sernin tried to pull it off. The priest hit his shoulder with the open palm of his hand. The abbot let out a strident scream and tried to scratch the priest. The knights of the Order of Saint-Jean and the canons started wrestling each other out of the room.

I rushed to my master and managed to take the coat off.

Either the horror of the scene that was unfolding about him, or the terror of not receiving the absolution had hastened the arrival of that force which takes a man's soul away. His eyes no longer solicited any pardon. When Hugues Jean and I leaned over their extinguished flame, they were nothing more than the mirror of the void.

* The origins of the Albigensian religion are obscure. One of the less known hypotheses is the one that attributes the apostle Bartholomew with the first foundations of the heresy.

VI

The count of Toulouse still awaits his burial*. The knights of the Order of Saint Jean of Jerusalem took him by force and placed him in an open coffin, in front of which the people of Toulouse flocked and wept. The bishop Foulque, however, enforced the ecclesiastical order forbidding the burial, in holy ground, for one who had been excommunicated by the pope. To the lamentations of the people, he answered that they had to wait for the pope to revoke his decision that, of course, never happened.

They then closed the coffin and it was moved from the reception room to a corner of their chapel, then to a more obscure corner in a little storeroom, where they kept the gardening tools.

During this period I meditated frequently on the manner in which events are chained together and on the destiny, which had presided over all my actions. As Marie the clothier had long ago prophesied, the evil that made my people suffer, had incarnated in three men; one dressed in red, one covered in steel and one who wore a mitre. I had, with my own hand, pierced the heart of the first one. My sister Aude had beheaded the second. Was it down to me to kill the third, who was by far the most evil.

Bishop Foulque feared the Toulousans' wrath and only came into the city for religious ceremonies. He lived in Verfeil castle, which Simon de Montfort had given him. Isarn Nébukat, the dispossessed lord had sought refuge in Toulouse and was secretly looking for partisans to take back his chateau and its domains. I went to find him. He was a wild and wily old wolf. I told him my plans but he laughed and said:

"Everything depends on what you expect me to pay." I told him that my name was Dalmas Rochemaure and this wasn't about money. He asked me again to fix a price. I decided not to bother with such a stupid man and made up my mind to act alone.

I went to stay in Verfeil under a false name. After a few days I knew the bishop's habits. He only went out with several men-at-arms. On the northern side of his chateau, down a slope, there was an Arabic garden planted solely with very ancient box trees. Now Foulque had a passion. He loved snails. He slept little and got up before the sun. Box trees, for some reason, harbor thousands of snails. At the break of dawn when the snails are loving the humidity of the morning dew, he wandered, armed with a basket, amongst the narrow alleys. When he had filled his basket, he returned to his chateau's terrace. He spread the snails out on the stones and played a mysterious game with them. No doubt he then ate them for lunch.

I had rented a room that I could leave without being seen by the blacksmith opposite. When the stars started fading, having put on a greenish jerkin and taken a sharpened blade, I climbed over the Episcopal garden wall. The box trees were thick and leafy and taller than a man. I hid myself amongst the branches, just off the central alley. It had rained a few hours earlier. Thousands of snails slithered around me. The box trees' perfume was melancholic and penetrating. Maybe it hid some magic. After half an hour I was drenched to the bone and singular images were presenting themselves before my eyes.

I never thought about Pierre de Castelnau, not even to rejoice for having chased him from the earth. Right across the Christian world the preachers had let it be known that when dying on the golden beach of the Rhône, he had only spoken words of forgiveness for his murderer. I never believed it. I saw him lying on the sand and I had the feeling that he was dying in silence. But now, in the middle of these wet box trees, with snails sliming all over me, I saw once more, in the same morning freshness, Pierre de Castelnau writhing with his opened chest.

Someone had leaned over him. A vague memory came back of his arm lifting to hold his companion by the neck. Maybe he had hurriedly whispered those words of forgiveness after all.

A pink beam began to bathe the aisle between the trees as the facts of this bizarre problem laid siege to my mind. What of it? If it was true? Was evil then not so inexorably separated from good? They followed different paths but forgiveness remained the supreme ideal in which everyone took refuge at the point of death.

A little noise ruptured the silence, no doubt a snail cracking under foot. In the still morning air, in the pinkening light, I distinguished bishop Foulque's silhouette. He was approaching with little steps, closely observing the ground. I pulled out my dagger still thinking about forgiveness and I put my finger on the tip to make sure it wasn't bent. Forgiveness was impossible for me. It was man's abdication, a cowardly approval of evil. But what if Pierre de Castelnau had really forgiven me?

Right next to me bishop Foulque bent down with great difficulty. He had shriveled. He was so old! His face was a yellowish bile-ridden mask. His love of snails, however, gave his gaze an unexpected flame. This flame became brighter as he had just spotted an especially big snail. Its tiny horns were pointing towards the sky as it lay on a branch the same height as my head. He stretched his hand out to reach it and spotted me.

He saw through the leaves a man ready to pounce but whose face must have reflected confusion. The naked blade though, left no doubt as to the intent. We were close enough to touch each other. My spirit was racing. I noticed just how hideous the bishop's face was. His sterile head was naked. His nose was budding. His cheeks were hanging. He had that inhumane extra-terrestrial expression that is brought on by the absolute and utter love of money*. I read, as if in a book, the thought he was having: What he had so feared was about to happen! An assassin had reached him. Shouting was useless.

Would he try to flee or just put the snail in the basket and pretend he hadn't seen anything?

Had Pierre de Castelnau really forgiven me? This dilemma was primordial. It felt insoluble. I planned the unrealistic project of finding the man in Rome who claimed to have heard the whispered forgiveness. Oh why hadn't I jumped down from my horse and bent over the fallen legate, close enough for him to bite me so that I might have taken away the certainty of his hatred with the mark of his teeth.

The bishop Foulque, staggering and clearly terrified, had taken a few paces up the alley, pretending to be calm. Then he dropped his basket and started running. I was a prisoner of the funereal enchantment of the box trees and memories. I watched him getting further away. I didn't have the slightest bit of pity for that old man, whose lifted robe showed his deformed and ridiculous legs, as if Tancrede, his executioner, had practised on them with his instruments. Not for one minute did I think of forgiving him for tormenting my city and my people. However I remained immobile, because another one like him, his evil brother, had forgiven me before dying, maybe.

The first shout for help he uttered woke me up. I took off down the narrow alleys, under the shadow of the box trees. By the time I had reached the part of the wall I had jumped over, no one had yet appeared at any of the widows. Thoughts change like life's images. Whilst running away, I was entirely preoccupied by the representation of the instrument of torture that Tancrede bragged about having invented. This instrument, to hasten the victim's confession, broke both arms and legs simultaneously. This gave me wings to cross the Verfeil forest. It made me cross the Tarn like a fish when its waters blocked my way.

As I was swimming against the current, I saw a white bird over head. It was flying in the same direction as me. I could not, however, work out what species it belonged to.

I thought of the dove that represented the Holy Ghost. Arriving on the other shore, I realized with sadness that my dagger had slipped out of its sheath and had been taken by the river*.

* He was never to be. The chronicler Aymeri de Peyrat writes, in the XIVth century, that rats ate the count's body. The coffin was still in the same place in the XVIth century. Bertrandi, author of Gestis Tolosanorum, saw the bones and noticed a fleur-de-lys shape on the posterior part of the skull. He estimated it to be natural and a presage that the count of Toulouse must have been joined to the French crown.

* Bishop Foulque had become so rich that when the king of France came to Toulouse, he welcomed him and his entire army in Verfeil.

VII

Bishop Foulque died peacefully in his bed in 1232. His last days were dedicated to writing poems to the Virgin Mary.

Wrapped in a shepherd's coat and mounted on a mule, I decided to leave Toulouse for good. Night had fallen and the autumn winds were blowing on the banks of the Garonne. A man had just lit the drawbridge's two lanterns. I heard him singing a song in my forefathers' tongue.

"Thank God! He's from Toulouse. I've nothing to fear from him." The Narbonnais gate's guard was a little further on. I could tell those northern men by their stature, seemingly cast out of a ridiculously outsized mold. I could see their hideous blonde beards, their swollen bellies full of beer and their strange halberds. In the middle of them sat a Dominican monk, one of the Inquisition's* minions who monitored the comings and goings. He looked at me with his sanctimonious cat's eyes. He didn't recognize me. Fooled by the empty jars that hung from the sides of my mule, he must have thought:

"He's a poor man returning to his village." He was only half wrong: I'm a poor man leaving my dearly beloved city where I was born.

I plunged down the dark road where the new moon made a profile of the poplars. How happy were these trees, solidly rooted in the earth and breathing the air, which has passed over Toulouse! I could hear the Garonne's water's along the banks of Pech David. I carried on a bit then, all of a sudden, I turned around. I could see the Daurade, the Dalbade and Saint-Sernin.

"Oh Toulouse! What have they done to you? I can see your houses, your lamps, your towers, but you are not the same. They've changed your soul. A foreign king's seneschal has more authority than your very own Capitouls. Raymond VII* has been robbed of his ancestor's city where that terrible Dominican sect now renders its own twisted and sick form of justice."

There were so many people accused of heresy that the Inquisition house overflowed and the neighboring streets were filled with prisoners waiting for their turn to be judged. The judges were worn out from so much condemning, but nevertheless they kept on, endlessly condemning. Night and day a groan rose from the tunnels under the Narbonnais castle. Blackened folk from Auvergne who looked like tree stumps and pot-bellied Normans with wily faces had installed themselves in the discerning and lettered Toulousans' palaces. The young no longer dared to sing their bawdy songs in the evening under the fig tree in the place des Carmes. The young girls dropped their Saracen colored dresses and took to wearing French fashions. They closed the baths, as it was now a sin to look after one's body. They burned the manuscripts of the Taur library because they enclosed some mysterious characters that possibly expressed an unholy wisdom. Where were the philosophers from Granada now, with their beards and turbans, who once gathered amongst the tombstones under Saint-Sernin's cypresses? Where were the Moorish musicians, who could vibrate the African desert sands with their darboukas? There was not a single Roman statue left standing. No longer – would any one dare to recite Plato out-loud.

"Oh Toulouse! I bid thee farewell. No longer will I hear the town crier announcing the arrival of the new wine. Nor laugh with the kids at the sight of an evaluation matron*. I'll no longer see the bread being weighed in front of the town hall. I feel, as I am about to lose them, how great these simple little pleasures were."

I carried on my way. The flanks of the Pyrénées were approaching. I reached the Ariege. Looking back I could no longer make out the contours of Toulouse's eternal mass.

Already the poplars had a different language. If I'd picked a fig, it would have tasted different. How cold the air turned as one moved further from Toulouse!

�֍

I sought shelter as a guest in Montsegur. From all the persecuted towns, the heretics who did not want to renounce their faith had come to Montsegur. On a mountain in the lands of Foix, surrounded by the gorges of the Ers and the Lectorier and protected by stone precipices, Esclarmonde, viscountess of Gimoez, had taken refuge in this impregnable castle.

Here I found all those faithful to the Cathar religion. There were the Canastbru with their fathers, their grandfathers, their sons and grandsons. There were the Malhorgas, blue eyed and hairy. There were the Nolasco, who are musicians, and fill the tower in which they are living with continuous music from their instruments. The western barbican was full of orphaned children. The soldiers camp in the courtyards under tents. The Parfaits were in the eastern donjon, and when they walk and meditate by starlight, the rays of their thoughts are so strong, that the donjon seems surrounded by a blue aura. There was a field of daisies which had been planted by the beautiful Alix d'Escaronia, and one could see her, watering can in her hand, accompanied by the gorgeous Pélégrina de Bruniquel, who took great care of a white rose bush.

Life in Montsegur also spreads underground in the forty-eight floors that are dug into the mountain. Subterranean rooms lined the stone galleries and their narrow embrasures opened onto the Ers gorge. At the bottom were the pools, the salt and wheat reserves, the jars of oil, in fact everything that Esclarmonde's foresight had decided to store in case of a siege. All the books and documents that were menaced by fire and destruction had been transported here one by one.

169

There were stables, forges, workshops and even grottoes for those who, on the path to perfection, reached it by the immobility of prayer. There were the deaconess' cells and the rooms where they met to form the mystic chain. The deaconesses were all women who had vowed themselves to chastity.

When, in the evening they came out in their white dresses and made a tour of the castle, I recognized amongst them some of Toulouse's courtesans next to ladies with illustrious names. Somewhere, but no one is sure where, the chosen one the invisible pope, elected by the Parfait's synod prayed and meditated. Esclarmonde de Foix resides, so they say, on the tallest tower, the one facing the Orient. When the nights were clear, people pointed at her silhouette cut out from the sky. An astrologer and a geomancer were always by her side. Both of them sought to understand the enigma of life and death by studying the earth and stars.

�֍

For a long time I didn't believe I was getting any older. I felt as strong as ever. I had neither the time nor the inclination to count my hairs, but I was sure they were as numerous as before. Only their whitening betrayed the passage of years. These were the mountains I had wandered when I'd run away from Mercus abbey, the torrents where I drank, and the trees under which I had fallen asleep. I had just rung the Tocsin, without knowing that this prophetic bell had announced the thousands of Tocsins that would ring out from the doomed towns, from the Rhône to Toulouse. I was young and happy then. I'm now getting older and somewhat wiser.

On the narrow path that I followed there were almond branches that I spread with my hands. It was hot and close to midday. Looking through the trees I saw a river running. I was walking alongside the Ers. I remembered meandering along this river long ago, under a similar sun. Was I on the same stretch of river?

No, most probably not, but the vegetation was the same. Frogs leap to the left and right and I took great care not to squash them, for little parcels of the divine soul are enclosed in all creatures. It was on the edge of the Ers that I had first caught sight of the miraculous shape of the sleeping Esclarmonde de Foix, on a little beach of golden sand.

What must she look like now? As Esclarmonde's spirit had become more perfect, had her flesh, which was the expression of it lost its beauty and become flaccid? Nobody was allowed to see her in Montsegur? She never came down from the tower where she lived. Maybe old age had ravaged her more than other women. Maybe she only had astral preoccupations. How sad was the law that beauty carried the secret of its death hidden in its essence! But are there no exceptions to this rule?

The branches in front of me were blocking the way. I spread them and then forcibly held back a shout. On a sand bank, a feminine figure lay under a half unfolded veil. Judging by the water evaporating from her skin she had just been swimming. She had three golden plaits. I saw her face and I recognized her. It was Esclarmonde de Foix! But how is this possible? She seems even younger than before. No doubt the movement of the branches woke her in an instant. I recognized the same steel in her eyes that struck mine when I carried her in my arms and had, for the first time, an understanding of the mystery of the spirit. Am I not the victim of some spell? Surely not for spells don't exist. Esclarmonde must possess that elusive secret of eternal youth.

A breath of wind, coming from I don't know where, passed over me. All of a sudden I took a step backwards and stepped back in time. I became a shaggy young man again, clothed in rags, whose feet were cracked and calloused from so much walking. I wanted to laugh, to run, and to ring the Tocsin for no reason. I felt that if I were thirsty I would have lapped the water instead of gathering it up in my hands. Obscure larvae have taken hold of my flesh, invoking the shades of the nether world.

171

I wanted to pounce and grab in my arms the one who, for all my life had symbolized spiritual perfection. To hold the tabernacle and profane it! I was surrounded by the smell of rosebay and sap. The earth seemed to be encouraging me. I threw myself forward. By coincidence I looked up and saw a white bird flying overhead. Is it a miracle? Is it the dove of the Holy Ghost? The bird flew down to the height of the treetops then disappeared, but I had received its message. I turned around and went back down the path.

In a few seconds I travelled through the years of my life. My hair that had darkened, whitened, my feet were no longer calloused. I strolled slowly towards Montsegur, towards its knights, towards its deaconess, towards its underground city, asking myself if I'd lived through a dream or reality, meditating upon Esclarmonde's eternal youth.

Some men, positioned on the highest points, signaled with flames by night and trumpets by day. Riders were endlessly using the road to Lavelanet. Those arriving from Foix and Toulouse were bringing bad news. Pierre des Arcis, seneschal to the king of France in Carcassonne, and the bishop of Albi had gathered an army that was currently still within Toulouse's ramparts. They had decided to destroy Montsegur, heretical hotbed that, from the top of its rock, stood up against the pope and France. Just as they had thirty years before they promised indulgences and blazoned crosses on their knights' chests' to stimulate their ardour.

From all over the Pyrénées the voluntary defenders came running. We could see them on the narrow snake like path that wound up to the castle gate. Some were peasants carrying their entire fortune on their backs, bags of flour or vegetables, others were knights who came only with their sword and lance.

Old Raymond de Pérelha, who was the lord of Montsegur stood on the threshold and welcomed them.

I'm amazed that such a large number of men, mules and horses could fit into Montsegur's subterranean galleries.

The taciturn Pierre Roger de Mirepoix was in charge of the soldiers. Dispossessed of his castle, in the darkness of a moonless night he went with a few knights to try and take it back. He failed and gave up and now his face was as resolutely shut as his lost fortress' door. I found Palauqui de Foix, Delga du Lauragais and Louis du Gers, next to whom I had fought in Toulouse. They were brave men and were the same age as me, but now they seem much older. The problem of time is a mystery.

I met the intrepid Loup de Foix and Jean Cambitor, the warrior magician with his double-edged shield. The front of his shield protected him from blows whilst the back was mirrored and with the point of his blade, he made ghosts appear. Roger de Massabrac was here too with his evil eye. He spoke to his friends from the side, but in the presence of his enemies, he faced them straight on and wide-eyed, because, he said it made them fall by the stillness of his gaze. Even the cranky Amaury Nebulat was here. Everyday, at midday, he threw his helmet down and tore off his clothes. He swore that he had to live naked to find true purity, the simplistic state of the first man.

Suddenly, wide-eyed I started trembling. A woman on horseback, who could have been taken for an adolescent, was advancing towards Montsegur's gate. She was wearing a sword, a silver helmet and was armed like a knight. I recognized the features of her face and the depths of her eyes. It was Esclarmonde de Foix, who had incarnated into my youth's ideal. I had obviously not dreamt when I saw her beside the river. The pure spirit had been obliged to take the sword and wear iron because of the hard times, but there she was, climbing towards Montsegur.

The young woman jumped lightly down from her horse. No sooner had she said a few words to Raymond de Pérelha than she began to search for someone else.

I had noticed with some surprise that the men who came in never failed to greet an insignificant little old lady sitting under a fig tree in the doorway of the interior courtyard. I'd hardly noticed her. Two men dressed in black stood at her sides. She was extraordinarily wrinkled and her dress was so simple that one would think it a servant's. It was her that the young woman was looking for. As soon as she saw her, she went and kneeled in front of her, respectfully kissing her hands. Who could the eternal Esclarmonde be prostrating herself to? I leant over to one of the numerous Canastbru sons who was standing next to me and asked him about the wrinkled old lady.

He looked at me, hurt and stupefied, as if he'd been insulted by a fool. He accused me of slandering the sacred. Then seeing my innocence, he said:

"That's Esclarmonde de Foix, viscountess of Gimoez, she came down for the first time today to greet her niece, Esclarmonde d'Alion." As all the Canastbru bristle with intelligence, he moved away sharply, clearly embarrassed to stand next to a man as ignorant as myself. I moved off even quicker. Once again I'd just felt the burning of a ripping wound. I needed to walk, to run, to externalise my disappointment.

Unhappy was he who believed in miracles, even the spiritual miracle. Nature was atrociously lacking in them. The laws of the flesh were inexorable. No divine force could install itself into a form that did not perish. Old age was stronger than spirit. My ideal chimera had been waning whilst I was creating her.

"Oh lord, if nothing remains, neither living forms, nor monuments, nor the images of gods, nor expression of perfection, then it is life, as my Albigensian brothers say, that is nothing but a bad illusion.

174

One must reject the succession of pains as quickly as possible, in order to attain the kingdom of true life where all is stable perfection and immutable love."

* The Inquisition's tribunal started in Toulouse in 1233. The first book burning provoked a popular uprising. A little later, the Narbonne council was obliged to beg the Inquisitors to reduce the convictions because there weren't enough materials in all the towns of the Midi for the construction of prisons.

* In 1229, the Paris treaty consecrated the deposition of Raymond VII. He submitted to the pope and the king of France. He flogged himself with a stick, as his father, Raymond VI had done in Saint-Gilles. He received the absolution. His estate would, upon his death, return to the crown.

* They were responsible, before a wedding, to see if the fiancée was 'all in order.'

VIII

In the circle of sheer mountains, between the ferruginous streams and silent pines, Montsegur, with its hermetic towers, looked like a tomb piercing the autumn sky. Pierre des Arcis' army slowly surrounded the plateau at the base of the precipices that lead up to the castle. On the stone esplanade that overhangs the Ers, we watched the banners floating, the crosses unfurling and we counted the machines of war, laughing at their tiny size. Night came, and as the stars lit up the sky, the valleys filled with fires.

I found myself standing alone in front of the castle. There was an old twisted oak that spread its branches over the abyss. A stone bench had been erected next to it and I sat down. This spot, however was being saved for someone of importance, for no sooner had I sat down, a hand touched me on the shoulder. I had barely time to stand up and fade into the shadows, when I saw Esclarmonde de Foix coming forward. A rumour has been spreading for several days that she was about to die. For me that was something that just didn't make sense. The Esclarmonde that lived within me died the moment I last saw her and wept. Every day, however, she slowly seemed to come back to life and I started to understand that the only ideal creatures are the ones that have neither face nor body, and are beyond death.

I watched the chatelaine of Montsegur taking little steps under the oak. I had thought that she was small, but now she seemed big. I could no longer see her wrinkles. She appeared to be carved out of a transparent ivory. The old lord of Pérelha had approached her and was consoling her of a pain unknown to me. They both leant forward, scrutinizing the darkness.

177

I overheard a word they keep repeating, the Holy Ghost, the spirit.... Then suddenly, I saw Esclarmonde twisting her hands and speaking to the stars as if they were her witness:

"My God! With a whole life, I've done nothing for truth, I've failed to serve the spirit."

Very close by a trumpet ruptured the silence. On the steep path that leads up to the castle six riders appeared. They must have been expected, for the watchmen waved their torches and shouted with joy. The door opened. I saw under their helmets, six male adolescent faces. They were Esclarmonde de Foix' and the viscount de Gimoez' six children. The lord of Pérelha spoke as she stepped towards them:

"See, you have been given an answer."

The siege of Montsegur had been going on for a month and I couldn't understand the mysterious drunkenness that reigned over the castle. At first I thought it was the ecstasy of war. But this happiness was very different to what I had felt or seen in my life amongst soldiers. It was a joy devoid of exterior manifestation, a pure soulful joy. It started spreading on the third day of the siege, when the rumour spread that Esclarmonde de Foix had died. This news was whispered from one to another, without commentary. It caused no apparent reaction. There was no collective prayer. No one knew in which part of the mountain her remains had been laid. Even in Montsegur they practiced the Cathar rite of secret burial, as had been their custom for a long time, due to the bishops insistence on violating the tombs of the heretics and the sanctity of death's slumber.

From that moment the gestures of my companions grew more feverish and their gazes were filled with sparkling light.

I understood nothing of their strange happiness. It was true the fortress seemed impregnable. Montsegur's triangular mountain was so vast, so bristling with precipices, that the royal troops could never be numerous enough to completely surround it but these considerations seemed insufficient to explain the current state of mind.

It was the jovial Arnaud Boubila who enlightened me. He was a portly and simple man who slept in the cell next to mine. He was so happy that I often heard him laughing to himself behind the partition that separated us. He had been a shepherd in his youth and was bottle-feeding a kid goat that he loved and slept with in his arms.

He loved the kudos of having been with Alfaro in the Avignonnet affair, where several Inquisitors had been murdered. He showed me with pride the stick with which, on the famous evening, he had cracked Raymond de Costiran's skull. Nick-named "the Scribe" he had drawn up such long lists of heretics to be burned that they couldn't be contained on any parchment.

Arnaud Boubila's greatest worry was that he couldn't take his stick with him when he died, for he wanted to present it to the Holy Ghost. Feeling pity for such a simple man, I assured him that the stick's ghost, with its murderous virtues, would not fail to accompany him.

One night, I heard Arnaud Boubila singing for longer than usual, then his kid bleated plaintively before falling quiet. I woke a while later with something humid on my hands. By the light of a candle, I saw that blood was running under the partition wall. I got up and went next door. Arnaud Boubila had killed his baby goat, and then he had opened his own veins. His stick was placed next to his heart.

"He's given himself the Endura," said the man in the next room when I went to wake him.

"He's happy now with his goat and his stick."

179

I understood from his longing gaze at the cuts in Boubila's wrists that he envied the shepherd's death and was thinking of the most practical way of imitating him.

What the Albigensians called Endura was the natural consequence of their philosophy. With life being evil, death became the happy deliverance. When the soul is free from remorse, free from passion, it is permitted to accelerate nature's course, and free itself from its bodily chains. This act, in truth, was reserved for Parfaits, but many simple believers, either to escape great pain or to accelerate the pleasure of the beatitude in a world without form, took their own lives. Esclarmonde's disappearance had given a mysterious signal and several Albigensians put an end to their lives in the same way as my neighbour. It was hoped in the first days of the siege that the crusaders would grow weary and leave. A rumour spread that the people of Toulouse and Albi were sending a rescue army. When it never arrived the lassitude began. Death, the marvelous death that opens the door to the world of light appeared very close, indeed somewhat inevitable. Everyone held their arms out towards it and called it with an ardent wish.

Holding hands, one evening in the setting sun, Jean de Cassenel and his two sisters threw themselves off the Ers' precipice. Bernard Ortolanus, put on a white robe and sitting amongst his children so as to give them a noble and useful example, pierced his heart with a dagger.

"He was wrong," said the wise Philippe Pellipar. "One shouldn't make it into a performance. You give death a reality by showing it. If you want to die you should just disappear."

And that very evening he disappeared.

Others believed you had to respect destiny, believing that everyone had a predestined time. It wasn't forbidden however to hasten that time by magical practices, by burning herbs and monotonous chanting.

180

In the underground galleries, on the towers and even when we made sorties, the Albigensians were waiting for their deaths with bated breath. One never knew if the one you left when you went to sleep wouldn't open his veins during the night. A silent calling drew my companions from their cells, galleries and donjons. The watchmen on the high towers were the ones who gave themselves the Endura with the greatest of ease, as the purer air and the clouds caressing them brought the beckoning mists and a foretaste of what they imagined lay beyond. Montsegur became the castle of death.

IX

Pierre Roger de Mirepoix hated me with an incomprehensible loathing, which he shared with his second in command, Jordain d'Elcongost. I'd always thought that it was because I'd shown heroism at least equal to theirs when we descended the castle's slopes, attacking the crusaders at random. I, for sure, didn't long for my death, but I fought with a calm indifference, a serene valour that must have inspired envy in these nervous and violent men. I was always sent to the most dangerous positions and charged with missions that expected the ultimate sacrifice. Daily miracles kept me alive but my companions pitied me, saying that I must have really bad luck to keep escaping the death they so desired. However, I was not of their opinion. At its root I could not destroy my taste for life and secretly rejoiced to see the sun rise on every new day.

All the war machines brought by the crusaders were too short. We saw on the slopes of Serrelongue, lumberjacks felling pine trees to build taller ones. Slowly, an enormous wooden tower rose in front of us. When the giant scaffolding was completely mounted, the tower started its ascent of the castle's steep slopes. It clung onto rocks, rocked over the folds in the land and for five months it climbed until its platforms, loaded with trebuchets and bricoles, were at the level of our towers. With the winter snows, a rain of arrows and an avalanche of rocks lashed down upon us. The crenels flew off. The dented barbicans trembled on their foundations. Gaping holes opened in the walls. The dead, the happy dead grew in numbers.

Help came to us from several castles.

On the darkest nights, a resolute troop, led by a guide, would manage to pierce the crusader's line and reach Montsegur. One time it was the architect Bertrand de la Baccalaria, with some Toulousan volunteers. He had the quixotic confidence of my people. He rubbed his hands wandering amongst the breached donjons and the crumbling walls, saying that the damage was trivial and could be repaired with ease. We trusted his genius and set to work. The castle, like its defenders, must have been possessed with a love of death. There must have been a will in the stones to remain a ruin. We only managed to rebuild makeshift walls and the towers kept crumbling down. The wood that should have served to lift the machines had rotted without apparent reason.

Another time it was Esclarmonde d'Alion who came to our aid with a handful of Aragonese riders. Eighty men had set out but only a dozen arrived. Esclarmonde d'Alion had come to kiss her love Jordain d'Elcongost. In Montsegur, all unions were mystical and there were only ideal embraces but this love was an exception to the rule. As the doors of the great gate slammed shut I saw Jordain's lips meet Esclarmonde's and in Montsegur's pure air, by the light of a flaming torch, that kiss burned brighter than the torch that lit it.

The attacks were getting more and more frequent and no one slept any more. The women and children ran to the most exposed area's hoping to be freed by a falling rock or a liberating arrow. The Parfaits stayed close to the fighters to give the consolamentum to the dying, freeing them from the chains of reincarnation. Most of them didn't actually need the Parfaits' magic blessing. They had already broken the last internal filament that bound them to the earth and they died with the certainty of being free.

It was when the situation became direst that Bertrand de la Baccalaria won most people over. A flame appeared one night at the summit of Bidorta. Everyone immediately thought that it was a signal from the king of Aragon. As the sun rose that spring morning, a lookout from the northern tower woke us shouting that he had just seen a huge army coming from Toulouse.

He had recognized Raymond's banner. In fact Raymond VII was at that moment prostrated at the pope's feet, as his father had before him in my company. There was no army. The lookout had been the victim of an illusion.

Apparitions tormented many of my companions. They kept seeing companions they had lost, that had been taken by the Ers' torrents, or that had disappeared in underground tombs. They lived amongst these shadows with a strange familiarity. Nora de Marcilhac was constantly conversing with the phantom of her sister India, who had died at the beginning of the siege. They had thrown themselves together down a precipice. Nora had been held back by her dress. She had seen it as a sign that destiny was forcing her to live. Since then her sister's ghost had stood beside her and her only worry was the impatience it showed that she carried on living. The Albigensian that had taken Arnaud Boubila's bed only lived in one half of the cell, maintaining that Arnaud Boubila still occupied the other. At night he heard the kid goat bleating and the stick that had crushed the skull of Avignonet's Inquisitor tapping.

The dead were neither painful nor annoying. They didn't demand to be avenged. They gently pushed their brothers and sisters to shed their earthly substance, to come and enjoy the state of love and fraternity without separation. I didn't manage, despite my keen hearing to hear their constant whispering. In-spite of my excellent eyesight, I never distinguished their contours. Everyone else saw and heard them and I'm sure they were not deceiving me.

The dead were sitting under every porch and mingling in every corridor. They filled the daisy field. A great number huddled under Pelegrina Bruniquel's roses. The doctors obtained secrets off them for the preparation of new of medicines. The children even got them to play in their games.

184

There was a point in the Ers gorge that was guarded by some crusaders from Mirepoix, who were still faithful to their old lord. A parfait spoke to them and it was agreed that one night they should let a few men and horses pass. Montsegur's treasure had to be saved. It was huge and had been gathered into a couple of rooms. There were riches in solid gold and precious objects from several Albigensian chateaux, whose lords had fled from Simon de Montfort. There were ancient manuscripts brought back from the Orient and most notably one from Manès himself written in Zend. There were the writings of Nicetas and somewhere the Parfaits had recorded the method that lead man towards perfection.

We loaded it all onto mules whose hooves had been covered in felt. Loup de Foix and Esclarmonde d'Alion commanded the few men, who in the case of an ambush, would fight to save the treasure.

From the top of the rocky balcony that overhangs the Ers I watched, with the group of leaders, the silent procession sink into the darkness. Esclarmonde d'Alion was last and in turning to wave at Jordain, she tripped and almost fell. Jordain watched as her silhouette disappeared. The Parfaits were following the Cathars' hope with their eyes.

Pierre Roger de Mirepoix, who stood next to me, thought about the gold that was moving further and further away. Had he not fought purely for its possession? His face expressed despair. Never had this man's enigma appeared so large. There wasn't a jot of Albigensian faith in him and he even scorned the believers for their scrupulous religion, their horror of spilt blood. He only believed in his own hatred. If Montsegur held so long, it was because of the will of this inexorable leader. He never confided in anyone. His only words were military orders. I felt he was linked to the castle's gold and when the gold had gone, he found himself in the middle of empty stones. He fought with the same tenacity, until its last hour, but maybe without knowing why.

185

Very late, when the dawn was about to rise, a flame on the mountains of Serrelongue showed us that the treasure was safe.

※

Roger de Massabrac had inspired too much confidence with the strength of his evil eye. He commanded the western part of the fortified mountain from a little bunker above a steep path. This path known only to the shepherds, was almost vertical. The stones were hostile and vertigo troubled the soul. It was understood to be impossible to climb it at night, especially with Roger de Massabrac's evil eye above you. No doubt a shepherd betrayed us. No doubt they found amongst the crusaders some particularly skilled mountaineers who possessed a talisman against the evil eye for it was by this path that our defeat crept towards us.

That day we had been attacked from all sides and were worn out. Bertrand de la Baccalaria made his evening round of the crumbling fortress saying how much better it all looked. We heard his joyful voice resonating through the ruins. We had barely started sleeping in the subterranean ants nest when the alarm trumpet sounded, closely followed by shouts. I grabbed my weapons and took off half dressed, barely taking the time to wake up my neighbour. The stairs I climbed spilled out onto the main courtyard where a torch was left to burn all night. By its light I saw Roger de Massabrac stumbling and leaning on the wall. I thought he had been drinking and was about to reprimand him when under a low door appeared a man I didn't recognize. He looked terrified glancing from left to right. I saw a red cross covering his chain-mail and everything he wore was shiny and new compared to the rags that adorned the defenders of the castle. In my folly I thought it was an incomprehensible disguise. Suddenly, he turned and shouted in French:

"Here, there are two here!" Leaping like a cat, he thrust his blade into Roger de Massabrac and then lunged at me. Roger de Massabrac fell flat on his face.

186

He was already dying when he received that final blow. I had time to see several wounds on his back. He must have got them as he was heading for the castle to sound the alarm. The man was still bounding, as if he were more feline than human. Albigensians came out from all sides. A few lances followed by gleaming eyes came out of the low door and we gathered on that side. A little group of crusaders with their backs against the tower's flank was exterminated in the shadows. Unfortunately they were not alone, they were swarming everywhere. Pierre Roger de Mirepoix had gathered the home guard that all slept in armour in the big hall in the central donjon. His voice had acquired a metallic tone. A warrior's genius animated him. He held a short spike in his right hand and a dagger in his left. He had thrown off his helmet as if he was sure he wouldn't be hit. Thanks to his cunning and foresight we were able to push back the enemy out of the circle of the four principle towers.

Then their enormous stone throwing machines, with much creaking and groaning started moving in spite of the darkness. There followed a rain of cyclopean blocks, as if the dark sky was against us and was dropping fragments of stars. A group of old men and children who had gathered underground came out singing and asking for death to come quickly, their wishes were granted. The men who should have been on our catapults had either been killed first or couldn't get up to the towers in the mayhem. We saw above us, the skeletons of our dislocated war machines struck with immobility. We couldn't work out what was burning or how the fire had been lit, but spirals of a suffocating smoke rendered us blind and blackened our faces. The Parfaits ran, blessing the dying with the consolamentum. Jordan du Mas Saint-Andréo whose chest had been opened, bid me farewell smiling and gave me an appointment in the other world where I was heading at a specific hour the following day. I saw Pelegrina de Bruniquel with an arrow in her heart, quickly bringing rose petals to her lips. All those who died cried:

"At last!"

Late in the night, there were a few minutes of calmness.

I was surprised to see Bertrand Marty coming towards me. He took me by the hand and led me through the wounded, along the interior staircase, to a little empty cell. Bertrand Marty was revered as the holiest of the Parfaits. My master Raymond VI venerated him. It was rumored that he was the pope of the invisible church.

"I've chosen you," he told me, "you must survive." I made a gesture expressing the impossibility of realizing this wish, but he stopped me:

"A brave man has to save the most precious part of the Albigensian treasure. You can still profit from the darkness, climb down the mountain and slip across the crusaders' lines. Do not regret death. It will not be the end for you. You have many human reincarnations to fulfill." Thus he assured me of an imperfection I knew well but that was nevertheless still unpleasant to have pointed out. It wasn't the right time for reluctant politeness and Bertrand Marty's purity obliged him to an absolute sincerity. He pulled out an oval object from his shirt. I half caught sight of it under the leather that surrounded it. It was a raw emerald that held a reddish liquid within it. He hesitated for a second. I wondered whether he was going to explain the nature of this treasure to me but instead he simply said:

"You must give this to the Parfaits who have taken refuge in the Ornolac caves. I trust you. God bless you." He then embraced me.

Montsegur's treasure had been transported to the Ornolac caves, near Castelverdun. I went back up the staircase thinking about how to get out of the castle.

In the main courtyard nearly all of Montsegur's defenders were gathered. Jourdain d'Elcongost was holding a torch above a clerk who was sat writing. Next to him Pierre Roger de Mirepoix shouted out names one after an other, his vibrant voice sounding strange. A lugubrious silence had fallen over the ranks of the crusaders. Dawn's first light was burgeoning. Whispering, I asked Delga what the significance of this scene might be.

188

He told me that the fighting was over. The whole mountain was full of crusaders. There were thousands of them. Pierre Roger de Mirepoix had made a treaty with the seneschal of Carcassonne. He had conceded what was left of the castle but had negotiated his soldiers' freedom. He had just written the list of soldiers who, with their weapons, were going to follow him out of the castle.

There were barely sixty soldiers still alive. Pierre Roger de Mirepoix gave the clerk the order to read the list that he had just written. As no one could hear him, he took the list back and read it himself, stopping to swear at the appalling handwriting. When he had finished, the clerk who had been standing up sat back down, livid. He wasn't on the list. My name too had not been read out, but as he was finishing, our eyes met. He hesitated, then articulated with regret:

"Dalmas Rochemaure."

The silence it left tore at my heart. We were going to leave three or four hundred Albigensians behind us, most of whom were the women and the aged. They had called for their death with such strength, that it had arrived, under the arched doorway, with lances and crosses.

Pierre Roger de Mirepoix told us to gather our weapons and hold them ready to defend ourselves, in case of treason. We lost a few minutes looking for a trumpet. All those who knew how to play it were already dead. The one who found the instrument produced only a note of eerie discordance. We descended the mountain, to the strange sound of this trumpet. The sun was rising. An unusual number of crows filled the skies. A group of cavalry preceded us with their sparkling armour. Another followed us. We were whispering that they were probably waiting to surround us and massacre us. The fatigue was such that even with this in mind several of my companions were sleepwalking. Jourdain d'Elcongost walked next to Pierre Roger de Mirepoix bitterly counting out the fighters that had been left behind.

"They're all dead," he answered with indifference.

At the bottom of the mountain, near the Ers, next to a wooden bridge there was a mass of cavalry standing to. Through the trees we glimpsed their tents where a fire was lit with a cauldron hanging over it and the soldiers who were on their break were looking up and laughing at us.

"They're going to come at us," my neighbour said pointing out the cavalry. Another murmured:

"The bridge has probably been sabotaged and will crumble as we pass." I saw Roger de Mirepoix's hand tightening on his dagger. Only Bertrand de la Baccalaria was completely reassured and said that the crusaders had prepared them a meal.

We passed the bridge. Nobody attacked us. The seneschal Pierre des Arcis was oozing chivalry. He was on horseback, leading a new group of cavalry. He watched us with curiosity, his head a little forward. He did not salute. He remained immobile but there was a nuance of emotion on his face and I'm sure he would have liked to shake our hands. Next to him was a fat man whose face lit up with happiness. It was Pierre Amiel, the archbishop of Narbonne, betrayed the previous year by his own canons as incapable, debauched and scandalous. He winked at us with goodwill as we passed.

We marched past without turning our heads, with all the dignity we could muster in our ridiculous garments. In truth we were sad to find such a sympathetic aspect to those we had so fervently hated during the whole year of the siege. The road to Lavelanet was crowded with chariots and mules. We took a little path that wound itself into the mountain.

After several hours walking we stopped on a rocky platform at the point where the path, having climbed the slopes of the Serrelongue, descended through a pine forest. In the distance the waters of the Ers were blue and metallic like the reflection of a sword. I saw some smoke spiraling upward in the depths of the valley. Looking back towards Montsegur I could make out the outline of an enormous pyre that had been erected on the platform called l'aire des Espagnols.

They had just lit it simultaneously from several sides and the flames started climbing into the still air. A circular forest of lances and helmets surrounded it. The neighbouring woods were full of men's silhouettes and reflections of armour. On the right, the bishops with their crosses and their clergy had formed a mass of gold and mitres. In front, the miserable hundreds that had remained in Montsegur were squashed so close together that they looked like a pile of palpitating human chain-mail. No noise reached us. A strange silence reigned that made it look more like an image, an arbitrary painting, than a living reality.

Suddenly, from an invisible signal, all the lances lowered as one, guiding the Albigensians towards the flames. I saw a man tearing off his clothes whilst gesticulating madly. It was midday. It was Nébulat. At last he was going to find the innocence of the first days. A few women ran to and fro. I saw others grabbing their children and covering their heads in the pleats of their dresses. Those who had so desired their deaths seemed to hesitate in front of it. The flame was now so immense it was rendered almost invisible in the sunlight, as if refined with another universe's hue. Then I heard an enormous choir, deep and religious. It was the Veni Creator. Started by the bishops, it was boomed out by the cavalry on their horses, by the lance bearers, by the whole army spread throughout the valley. Maybe there was some mysterious death call heard by my heretical brothers and sisters in the song. As if the pyre was nothing more than the door by which one enters the divine lands, they threw themselves into its seething portal as one. The Veni Creator grew until it echoed off the mountains and resonated amidst the pines.

I noticed Pierre Roger de Mirepoix was standing next to me, watching his companions burn. He was stone-faced. Was he dreaming of revenge? Did he regret not having died fighting in Montsegur's ruins? I tried to talk to him, but he did not answer. As I was no longer dependent on him I thought about severely reproaching him for his hard heart. He would probably have tried to kill me. On reflection I thought that closed and mute souls were best left to their shadows. We were both worn out and fell asleep side-by-side*.

�֍

*All Montsegur's prisoners were not burnt. A small number including Raymond de Pérelha, were sent to Carcassonne's prisons where through torture the inquisitors forced them to denounce other Albigensians.

X

The entrance to the grotto of Ornolac* is in the flanks of the rocky mountain, at the point where the Ariège receives Ussat's springs. Its underground labyrinths extend to measureless depths. There are galleries that descend, others that climb, vaulted ceilings taller than any cathedral and at the heart of its shadows, a lake of silent waters. It was in this cave that the last of the Albigensians, pursued across the lands of Foix, took refuge one by one.

For a while I lived with the shepherds. Then I received hospitality from Alion castle before it was burned down. The seneschal of Carcassonne destroyed all the heretical lords' castles. In order to avoid certain death many Albigensians renounced their faith. The rest of us became partisans and lead the resistance in the mountains. Eventually we became too few to fight, so I too went underground into Ornolac.

Those who had been there a long time had grown accustomed to life without light and were consumed in perpetual prayer. Pierre Pagès had succeeded Bertrand Marty and it was into his hands that I placed the precious stone that had been entrusted to me in Montsegur. In the darkness of this cave, where there was no vegetation, no birds, in the trembling candlelight I recognized faces I had seen before but had then forgotten. I saw a labourer from Carcassonne who had been under my command during the siege of that city. I saw Pierre de Roaix de Toulouse's nephew and Ferrocas the peasant who understood nothing but was full of love.

The seneschal's soldiers were tightening the ring they had formed around the entrance to the cave.

We learned that all the paths in the lands of Castelverdun were guarded. Pirogues filled with armed men patrolled the Ariège. The L'Hermit and Bedaillac caves had been stormed and the inhabitants massacred. The last runners who managed to reach us announced that the seneschal had decided to storm Ornolac.

I was surrounded by men, worn out and discouraged by the miseries of their errant life. Their energy was shattered. They expected nothing from this world and only aspired to the happiness beyond. I did, however, manage to gather the most audacious ones. I stationed them overlooking a narrow bend between two galleries. The position of the rocks and the incline of the tunnel made it a very easy place to defend. The first soldiers who appeared were pierced by arrows sprung from the shadows. The seneschal quickly made his men retreat. No doubt he knew the length of the galleries and understood the difficulty of pursuing us. And so it came to him to use another, surer way.

All the Albigensians were gathered in a great hall, as tall as a church. It was here that the treasure and the provisions were kept. Here the same little oil lamps could serve everyone. Light was the rarest of things in Ornolac as the oil and wicks were in short supply. The Parfaits, charged with the distribution, did so with whimpering pleas for economy. A few families and hermits had bedded down in remote corridors that led lord knows where, to meditate or to die alone. We never found out what happened to them. All the rest were gathered in the central chamber, hoping to find together the necessary strength of soul to stave off the fear of darkness. In order not to reveal our whereabouts, we could only pray or talk in hushed voices. This constant whispering, with the flickering of small flames under the vaulted rocks, rendered our assembly even more lugubrious.

All of a sudden the sound of rocks being moved ruptured the silence. The walls vibrated around us. Those who were guarding the cave's entrance ran up and told us, panting, that they had started to build a wall across the entrance.

Everyone stood up and rushed to see the sun for the last time. Some even considered giving themselves up, then they stopped, remembering the prisons of Foix and the torture rooms where their companions had perished in slow agony. The Albigensians sat back down in the darkness, formulating a silent farewell to the sun.

Light is a world of shining beauty that none can be forced to forget. When, after some hours, we no longer heard the blocks piling up and the builders' work stopped, despair engulfed the interred. Cries rang out. Men, up till then quiet and resigned became furious. A few lost their minds, running hither and thither, dashing their heads against the rocks. Others, whose rage made them even more nonsensical, tipped over the precious lamp oil.

Pierre Pagès and the wise ones wandered from group to group, trying with their words to attenuate the pain. Without a remedy for darkness they spoke of the spiritual sun that each of us carries in our soul, of the Holy-Ghost's marvelous light. Everyone tried to imagine that internal source of luminescence forever lost but the humid air and the shadows of the cavern's mysterious dome rested so heavily upon us that hope couldn't take hold. Our thoughts could only conjure crepuscular ghosts of the sun, which dissipated as soon as they were born.

With unimaginable strength a young child repeated to its mother:

"I want to see! Take me to where I can see!" This shout, which expressed the common desire, multiplied the anguish so much that several proposed chasing the mother and child down a corridor, far enough away for the cries to be inaudible.

I kept noticing Pierre Pagès' chest glowing strangely when he walked. I asked him about it. It was there he carried the stone containing the trembling reddish drops wrapped in a leather hide.

"It's Christ's blood," he told me, "which was preserved in Césarée and was then transported to Gènes.

Some faithful Albigensians received it as proof of the truth of which they are the trustees. When you feel your strength failing and death around the corner, stare at this stone and your soul will be lightened."

I cannot evaluate either the time that passed, or the life that ebbed out of us. I know that many died very quickly, mostly due to the lack of sun. At the beginning we took their bodies very far away to the end of a gallery, and left a little lamp next to them. But our strength must have faded for we soon carried the dead less far and left no light.

A few Parfaits were in charge of the distribution of food. At first they did so with economy and wisdom. Then a lassitude took hold of them and they stopped making sure it was evenly distributed. Some thought of bringing death closer by starving themselves. Others sought the same result from eating too much. Then there were those who took what they could and put it in places for later, which they promptly forgot and could never find again.

We went to fetch water from the lake and brought it back in pitchers. It was icy and tasted of chalk. This water, drunk in abundance was perhaps the cause of the mysterious poisoning that many died of. The sides of the lake were impressive. It must have rested in fluorescent rocks as it gave off a vague greenish light, like the dead sun of some hellish netherworld. We only went there in numbers and talked loudly to quell our fears of these stygian waters.

A brave hermit climbing along the walls, had managed to reach the other side of the lake. We saw him in the position of prayer. He was awaiting his death. From afar he waved his hand when he saw us. Then he stopped waving his hand. He was a taller than average man and from this distance his silhouette took on a grotesque and menacing appearance. A few of my companions reckoned that he had grown every time we came back. This phantasmal elongating dead hermit increased the terror that the lake inspired.

Lethargy took hold of Ornolac's living buried.

196

Two or three young men who had gone through the dark galleries, came back swearing that if they had walked for a long time in a Northerly direction and found a narrow corridor whose extremity was lit by daylight. They had taken care to mark the way and offered to take anyone wishing to follow them but nobody got up. Life on earth had become impossible for anyone wishing to keep their faith. Besides, the lethargy was too great. It was better to die in the absence of effort. Everyone had given up hope of ever seeing the sun again.

We also had to do without the modest oil light. The little lamps went out one after another. As the last one's light was weakening, I considered the faces of the creatures leaning over the clay lamp where the protected wick expired. Amongst these faces, I recognized Esclarmonde d'Alion. Her face was different, a little puffed up. The suffering of an unhappy life had hardened her gaze, disfigured her perfect oval features. The familiar graciousness of her expression was still there but it floated like a mist that was about to disappear. The form, which had embodied my image of the incarnation of perfection, had lost its purity and it was the last image I saw before being enveloped by the darkness.

There was a soundless shudder as the lamp's final feeble glow climbed up to the sepulchral roof of the vault, to die amidst the stalactites. I sat down, prey to a distress greater than the fear of death. Much later, someone called to me from across the darkness. Fumbling, I tried to make my way towards them, tripping over fallen bodies, touching stiff limbs and marble faces. The small number who remained alive had resolved to form a circle around Pierre Pagès and to die holding hands. I took my place in this chain and heard a monotonous chant as the brethren transmitted their prayers to one another. I didn't understand the meaning of the prayers and their words died on my closed heart.

Maybe an hour or maybe a day later, in the state of semi-consciousness into which I had fallen, images started to appear and unfold before me.

197

They were at first pleasant scenes that had made me laugh in my childhood. Then came the people that I had known, who must have been somewhere in Toulouse or elsewhere and others who perhaps already belonged to the kingdom of death that I was about to enter. Strangely, I could remember all their names, as if they had carried it written on their foreheads. They moved around in a circle whose axis was that blurred glow which came from Jesus Christ's coagulated blood and hung around Pierre Pagès' chest. That miraculous light fascinated me, as it was turning a more and more fluorescent shade of ineffable, emerald green.

I marveled that a man as ordinary as I, with such coarse passions, had been chosen to save the divine blood and carry it underground, into the midst of His faithful elect. I'd always shown a somewhat mediocre intelligence, only dimly understanding the highbrow conversations that the wise men had held in front of me. Now there came a belated regret at not having chosen a more spiritual path. At the same time as that regret, as a sort of prize for having felt it, my understanding grew, and the opaque veil that had so long blinded me was torn away.

Words that I had heard and misunderstood in the past came back to me loaded with meaning. Obscure theories unfolded with sudden clarity. I was filled with gratitude for certain characters, as I understood their role, and the second I thought of them, they seemed to appear before me. I saw the philosophers who had searched for the meaning of life. I saw Basilide, I saw Valentine, all the Gnostics with their luminous abstractions. The Alexandrines were exposing the philosophy of divine emanations. I understood why Barthelemy had kept his teachings secret, why Manès had been skinned alive, why Hypacia had been stoned to death. I understood the purpose of Nicetas' journeys and why he had thought that Toulouse should be the point on earth from which truth would shine. I especially liked Nicetas for that legitimate choice. I understood what I had never comprehended. The Holy Ghost was nothing less than man's union with infinite intelligence.

198

I was swimming in the incomparable joy of having become enlightened after a lifetime of ignorance when, dissipating all the other images, a man in a white robe appeared. I recognized Pope Innocent, who been dead a long time. He was walking quickly, his eyes fixed on me, as I had seen him before, in Saint-Jean's basilica. I felt the same surprise and terror. All of a sudden, he bent over and with an extraordinarily easy gesture he conjured away Pierre Pagès' emerald.

"All relics belong to the church," he told me. His face was filled with something beyond cunning, that innate ability to make the most of things. He shook his tiara of symbolic peacock feathers and pointing them out with his finger, he said:

"I see with all these eyes. I see all the heresies that appear on earth and I suffocate them all." Basilide, Valentine, Manès and Nicetas were standing either side of him holding little candles. With one breath Innocent blew them out, as if to illustrate his words. Around me the dead Albigensians struggled to their feet, holding out their flickering lamps. Protecting them with their hands they tried to raise the flames, but Innocent shook his robe and they all went out. I heard his severe voice addressing me:

"Do you finally understand, Dalmas Rochemaure? I extinguish all spiritual light that does not come from the Church. No one has the right to make up their own God. I forbid it. Even reading the Scriptures is forbidden, as man would inevitably discuss their meaning while studying them. My power is to congeal, to coagulate, and to turn to stone. And pity the rebel! I'm always the winner and I'll bury all who stand against me, in a basilica of darkness..."

Yes, I understood. Everything was made clear to me. I was, in fact, already in that monstrous, shadowy cathedral, haunted by the heretics' ghosts, by those who had discussed the dogma, attempting to light the lamp of their own truth. Pope Innocent was now celebrating an inconceivable mass, oblivious of my presence and the unavailing shadows.

199

The basilica was as vast as the planet. The altar, the burned out candles, the cult's symbols, everything was carved out of an obscure porphyry. From all the corridors came mica eyed, marble-like cardinals. I saw the pontiff's solid back from which emanated his love for everything hard, unchangeable and inert. He stood up in the shadows and lifted a mineral host.

Suddenly, I was seized with a taste for subtle and weightless ethereal things. I wanted to bathe in the clouds, to float in the unimaginable ethers. On both sides I held hands with my dead companions. Then, I severed the funereal chain. Silently I dressed with a thousand precautions, taking great care not to interrupt the inanimate ritual. My desire to escape this terrestrial concentration of matter was so great that I then lunged into the darkness. Falling down only to get back up and carry on.

Around me, I felt the cave's walls were solidifying into something denser than any known earthly element. The stalagmite pillars shriveled and I saw the rocks petrify in the dome that was lowering to crush me. Everything was moving. Liquids were mutating into mud. Mud solidifying. I felt the currents of lower, denser vibrations as if nature were working in reverse. Innocent III, with open arms, became one with his material substance and turned into a stone pope. Enlightened to the point of weightlessness, I fled. My rekindled spirit drove me and gave me its power, stronger than death. I remembered some young men had spoken of a gallery where they had seen sunlight, somewhere to the North. I had no trouble heading in that direction. I'd made an evening habit of facing towards Toulouse, regardless of where I was. That favorably attractive city was to the North of the Ornolac caves and it was in that direction that I had turned when I had lain down to die.

I clambered over the fallen bodies and my first bounds carried me to the lake. I walked along the bank, noticing that the hermit had fallen over. It didn't seem important. I was lifted by a force emanating from a source in the deepest part of me. My life had been a game, a series of insignificant acts.

I had devoted myself to my people and yet had done very little for them. It was now that my mission was about to begin. I had just received a mysterious gift. I was possessed with such a desire to communicate that I started debating with myself whilst I was running. An unexpected intelligence had fallen on me as if those who had departed had left me their thoughts as gifts. I was proud of this heritage and it needed propagating. It was my responsibility to tell the world the history of my brothers, the history of the entombed truth and resuscitate this message, as precious as Jesus Christ's blood, found in Césarée.

I didn't have the impression of walking for very long. At a crossroad, where the corridors narrowed, a snake slithered out in front of me and showed me the way. I saw far in the distance the moon's inimitable clarity. The corridor, however, was obstructed by scree. There was a crack where the clay had resisted; where the re-fluxing matter was endowed with an inner force. I had to lie flat on my stomach. I slithered like the snake, holding onto rocks, I fought against the living molecules of the primordial substance, which were combining to suffocate me. At last, I felt roots in my hands and bats flew out in front of me. I had escaped the embracing matter.

The icy waters of the Ariege ran at my feet. The moon beamed in the infinite vault of the heavens. I fell to my knees and spread my arms towards the light. It felt as if it were a symbol for my people. The evil ones had tried to bury us alive, but we would never cease holding our arms out to the moon's spirit.

❈

•This cave is now called Lombrive, close to Ussat in the Ariège.

Epilogue

Glory to the winged words that resuscitate the dead by coming to life for the living and by conjuring their forefather's faces!

Glory to the magic words that propel men's actions across time, making them more memorable than those of the three judges, sat in their erstwhile hell!

Glory to the archangelic words that tear open the forgotten shadows! Silence is evil's most powerful weapon. Evil passed over my country and it left behind silence and its companion, fear. Half a century sufficed for the men of the Midi who suffered both physically and spiritually to virtually forget the history of their pain.

Leaning on a stick, with my head of white hair, and my trailing beard, I wander from village to village. They think that I am begging, but in reality I am giving. I'm giving them their stolen memories.

By a singular curve I regained the folly of my youth. It is thanks to this that I feel so alive. The abbey's priors have all changed. Everywhere there are new marshals and seneschals from France. No one of importance knows me. Who would think of imprisoning an old man who dances in the street when he sees a happy child and grossly prostrates himself in front of a passing Inquisitor?

Every-time I see a man sleeping next to his jug of milk, I pour it over him. When I walk past a bell, I rush in and pull the rope to hear it ring.

With great care I search in every village for the ones who are susceptible to hear my story to the end. I never address those who have children. The state of parenthood renders a hostility to all that is out of the social order and the established religion. I also don't address the intellectuals. I prefer to choose someone naïve, whose eyes are filled with wonder, because the naive have more faith than the intellectuals. I tell them how flourishing and beautiful the Midi was before the French had arrived. How the men of letters were honored, how thought reflecting in matter, naturally became beauty.

I tell them of the death of Béziers, of Carcassonne and Toulouse. I show them how a city can perish, yet keep its palaces and spires. I try to explain how such an injustice can stay alive, endlessly multiplying its effects, until one day it is honoured by those who committed it and then forgiven by those who suffered it. It is the act of forgiveness that is the hardest to understand. Vengeance's beauty is so easily accessible!   It seems to have a brave sort of nobility.

Vengeance is the first thought that comes to the faithful who hear what I have to say. They immediately talk of killing. I struggle to explain to them that one dead man is chained to another, with as much strength as a son to his father, and all these corpses form a chain that will be endless, unless it is broken by an act as surprisingly simple as a pardon.

Saying this I am in conflict, as I do not fully understand the pardon that the Albigensians prescribed. What does it matter if I don't comprehend the inner meaning of the message? It suffices that the message is passed on whether I understand it or not.

I will teach it forever. As Bertrand Marty told me, my imperfection will force me time and again to return to earth and take on new human forms. In every one of those forms I will recall the terrible forgotten history. They burned the books, the holy texts and all the testimonies of Albigensian thought.

They rebuilt the stone towers and sculpted caricatures of saints in the place of Greek goddesses but I will never tire of breaking this malign silence.

I will evoke the fallen towers of old, the vanished chapter house, with its Capitouls and their ivory sticks and the Saint-Sernin cemetery where the dynasty of the Raymond Saint-Gilles rest.

I will make the dead live again, as long as they are not permitted to rest in peace. So that they might find oblivion from the evils of the past and their animistic souls can serenely leave their bones.

I will claim a Toulousan body with each successive wave of incarnation. My effort will be constant, my sincerity full of light, and my love for my brothers ever growing.

May my future incarnations be more clairvoyant and wiser, filled of finer matter like the wine from the hills of Pech David that purify with time.

May the pointed edge of my words cast an ever-increasing incandescent light?

May those words, animated with life, become more perfect and more full of truth so that I might be able to set my eyes on Toulouse once more, without seeing the Albigensian's blood in the color of her red bricks, so that injustice is wiped from the hearts of the unjust and their pardon understood by those who give it.

�֎

Acknowledgements

Maurice Magre (Le Sang de Toulouse)
Miss Scarlet (www.shadowtheatre13.com)
Richard Stanley (Hardware, Dust Devil, The Secret Glory and many more)
John Redhead (…and one for the crow, Soft Explosive Hard Embrace, etc.)
Martin Lowe (Secretary to the Scottish Theosophical Society)
Joanna Bourne (www.joannabourne.co.uk)

Published by Goosecroft Publications, 5 Cecil Aldin Drive
Purley on Thames, Berkshire, RG31 6YP, England

First published March 2011
ISBN: 978-0-9566341-2-2
Designed and typeset by James Edward Bourne

Printed and bound in the UK by Anthony Rowe

www.ingramcontent.com/pod-product-compliance
Lightning Source LLC
Chambersburg PA
CBHW071950090426
42740CB00011B/1886